Template-Free™
QUILTS AND BORDERS
by Trudie Hughes

ACKNOWLEDGMENTS

My special thanks to:

Marie Shirer, for lending me designs when I need them.
Judy Martin, for her permission to let me use her June Bride block, which first appeared in her *Ultimate Book of Quilt Block Patterns*.
All the fabric companies, for creating fabrics that excite me and keep me sewing.
The staff at Patched Works, who work around me, over me, and despite me.
My new Compaq 386 and Bernina 1030, for keeping up with me.

CREDITS

Photography ....Brent Kane
Cover photo ....Fred Milke
Graphic Art and Illustration ....Stephanie Benson
                                                                              Barb Tourtillotte
Text and Cover Design ....Judy Petry
Editor ....Liz McGehee

Template-Free Quilts and Borders ©
©1990 by Trudie Hughes
That Patchwork Place, Inc.
P.O. Box 118, Bothell, WA 98041-0118

Printed in the United States of America
97 96 95 94 93 92 91   6 5

Library of Congress Cataloging-in-Publication Data

Hughes, Trudie.
    Template-free quilts and borders : book 4 / Trudie Hughes.
        p. cm.
    "B-111"--Cover.
    ISBN 0-943574-64-1
    1. Quilting--Patterns. I. Title.
TT835.H843 1990
746.46--dc20   89-20677
                                                          CIP

Contents

Introduction

Template-Free™ Quilts and Borders is the fourth book in my *Template-Free™ Quiltmaking Series*. For the past twelve years, I have enjoyed teaching these fast, accurate techniques to quilters of all skill levels, from beginning to advanced. Quilting is a lifelong study for me, and I am constantly working on new skills. With skill comes confidence, and once you have confidence, you gain speed.

Template-Free™ Quilts and Borders presents six new quilt designs, with detailed step-by-step directions and diagrams for thirteen quilts in a variety of sizes. Each quilt is an exercise in a particular technique. It may be a difficult piecing problem or the cutting of a new shape. Soon you will be able to adapt template designs to the rotary cutter, and design sources that you once overlooked will take on new possibilities.

The quilt patterns were selected for new challenges. I have always been intrigued with diagonally set designs that feature pieced setting triangles, so you will find a few of these in this book. A Gallery of color photos, which hopefully will inspire you, begins on page 43.

All readers will want to familiarize themselves with the information found in Getting Started on page 5. It provides valuable details on yardage and a sewing test that will aid in your accuracy.

Following the quilt patterns, you will find ideas for eighteen pieced borders, and I will share my techniques for planning these borders. A simple work sheet will help you to rotary cut the borders and change them to fit the particular quilt you are making. A review of borders from all my *Template-Free Quiltmaking* books is included, along with helpful information to aid you in adapting these borders to other quilts.

For those unfamiliar with template-free quiltmaking, or those needing a refresher course, there is a review section found at the end of this book. It provides detailed information on the various cutting techniques.

Getting Started

Before you begin sewing these quilts, you need to be aware that the most important skill needed for successful results is maintaining the proper seam allowance. For this reason, I think it is a good practice to take my sewing test.

Sewing Test

Take three strips of fabric, 1½" wide by about 5" long, and stitch together, side by side.

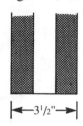

They should now measure 3½" from raw edge to raw edge. In machine piecing, the seams are pressed in the same direction. A slight amount is lost in the seam. What is most important is that segments turn out the right size. Therefore, you will find that "scant" ¼" seams work best. This simple test will help you find where to sew.

Featured Unit

Sometimes a particular unit becomes a challenge in machine piecing. The more you practice executing it, the easier it becomes. In this book, I am introducing a new unit. This featured unit will appear in many quilts, either in the basic design or in the pieced border. Sometimes the featured unit looks like this:

Other times it looks like this:

I found it helps to sew with the small triangle as the underneath layer, press, then add the other triangle.

Yardage Requirements

In planning the yardage requirements for the quilts in this book, I figured all fabric to have 40 usable inches. Once the yardage was calculated, I rounded it up to the nearest fraction of a yard. Although fabric is listed and sold as 45" wide, normally you will have only 40–42 usable inches. If you do have 45 usable inches of fabric, you will probably have extra yardage.

Since I own a quilt shop, I have seen what happens when your yardage is figured too closely. Most quilters would rather have a little bit left over to add to a scrap quilt or as a fudge factor, in case something is cut incorrectly. Several quilts in my books make use of these leftovers.

In the yardage requirements, fabric is broken down as to function. That way, you can substitute different fabrics for the border, binding, etc. You may not want to add the pieced borders, so you can easily eliminate that yardage.

All cutting directions are based on strips cut crosswise, selvage to selvage. I have found that the most efficient way to cut shapes from strips is to fold strips only once. Several strips can be layered and cut.

Note: Cutting instructions have been written in the shortest possible form. When cutting instructions tell you to "cut 5 strips 3" wide," this means each strip should be cut 3" wide.

In figuring the yardage for the backs of these quilts, I tried to plan the most efficient use of fabric. Therefore, sometimes it is pieced cross-grain, and sometimes it is pieced lengthwise.

Quilt Patterns
COUNTY LINE

Fabric A   Fabric B   Fabric C   Fabric D   Fabric E

This design is simple to piece and to select fabric for. It requires six fabrics, shaded dark to light. The easiest strategy in selecting fabric is to use a monochromatic scheme.

Lesson: Sewing consistent seam allowances. At one point, you will have a strip with five seams. Sewing inaccurate seams will alter the block measurement.

Crib Quilt

Block size: 18"
Number of blocks: 6 blocks, set 2 by 3
Pieced area finishes to 36" x 54".
After first border, quilt will be 39" x 57".
After last border, quilt will be 44" x 62".

FABRIC REQUIREMENTS

45" wide fabric (see page 5)
³/₄ yd. each of 6 fabrics, shaded dark to light
First border: ¹/₂ yd.
Last border: ¹/₂ yd.
Backing: 3 yds. (pieced crosswise)
Binding: ¹/₂ yd.

CUTTING REQUIREMENTS

Fabric A (Darkest)
1. Cut 2 strips 8" wide.
2. Cut 2 strips 2" wide.

Fabric B (Darker)
1. Cut 2 strips 6¹/₂" wide.
2. Cut 4 strips 2" wide.

Fabric C (Dark)
1. Cut 2 strips 5" wide.
2. Cut 6 strips 2" wide.

Fabric D (Light)
1. Cut 2 strips 3¹/₂" wide.
2. Cut 8 strips 2" wide.

Fabric E (Lighter)
Cut 12 strips 2" wide.

Fabric F (Lightest)
Cut 12 strips 2" wide.

First Border
Cut 5 strips 2" wide for
  first border.

Second Border
Cut 6 strips 3" wide for
  last border.

Binding
Cut 6 strips 2¹/₂" wide.

PIECING AND ASSEMBLY

Blocks
1. Make 2 set-ups of the following strips:

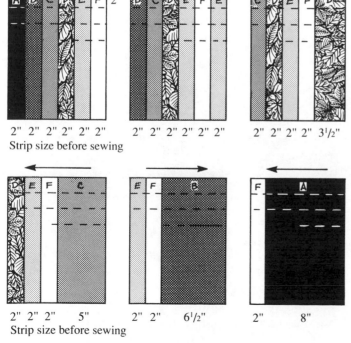

2" 2" 2" 2" 2" 2"
Strip size before sewing

2" 2" 2" 2" 2"

2" 2" 2" 2" 3¹/₂"

2" 2" 2" 5"
Strip size before sewing

2" 2" 6¹/₂"

2" 8"

Arrows indicate direction in which seams should be pressed. Each of these set-ups should measure 9¹/₂" from raw edge to raw edge.

2. Place rows 1 and 2 right sides together, rows 3 and 4 right sides together, and rows 5 and 6 right sides together. Cut every 2". You will find all seam allowances going in opposite directions! Make 24 cuts. Assemble these pairs into 24 blocks that look like this:

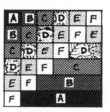

After blocks are completed, press seams toward row 6. These blocks should measure 9¹/₂" from raw edge to raw edge.

3. Four smaller blocks make up a major block. Make 6 blocks that look like this:

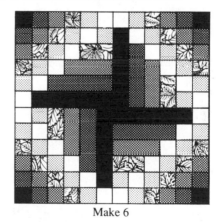

Make 6

4. Following illustration, assemble in rows.

Borders and Finishing
1. After pieced area is completed, add first border. With 2" strips of first border fabric, measure off 2 strips, each 36¹/₂" long, and sew to top and bottom. Press. Piece the remaining 2" strips on the slant and measure off 2 strips, each 57¹/₂" long. Sew to long sides; press.

2. Add second border. With 3" strips of second border fabric, measure off 2 strips, each 39¹/₂" long, and sew to top and bottom. Press. Piece the remaining 3" strips on the slant and measure off 2 strips, each 62¹/₂" long. Sew to long sides; press.

3. Layer, quilt, and bind.

Lap Quilt

Fabric A	■	Fabric D	🍂
Fabric B	▦	Fabric E	▫
Fabric C	▨	Fabric F	□

Block size: 18"
Number of blocks: 12 blocks, set 3 by 4
Pieced area finishes to 54" x 72".
After border, quilt will be 60" x 78".

FABRIC REQUIREMENTS

45" wide fabric (see page 5)
1⅛ yds. each of 6 fabrics, shaded from very dark to
    very light
Border: 1 yd.
Backing: 4¾ yds.
Binding: ¾ yd.

CUTTING INSTRUCTIONS

Fabric A (Darkest)
1. Cut 3 strips 8" wide.
2. Cut 3 strips 2" wide.

Fabric B (Darker)
1. Cut 3 strips 6½" wide.
2. Cut 6 strips 2" wide.

Fabric C (Dark)
1. Cut 3 strips 5" wide.
2. Cut 9 strips 2" wide.

Fabric D (Light)
1. Cut 3 strips 3½" wide.
2. Cut 12 strips 2" wide.

Fabric E (Lighter)
Cut 18 strips 2" wide.

Fabric F (Lightest)
Cut 18 strips 2" wide.

Border
Cut 7 strips 3½" wide.

Binding
Cut 7 strips 2½" wide.

PIECING AND ASSEMBLY

Blocks
1. Make 3 set-ups of the following strips:

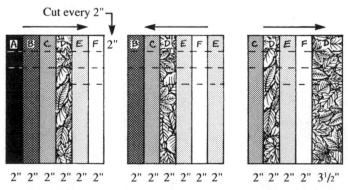

2" 2" 2" 2" 2" 2"   2" 2" 2" 2" 2" 2"   2" 2" 2" 2" 3½"

Strip size before sewing

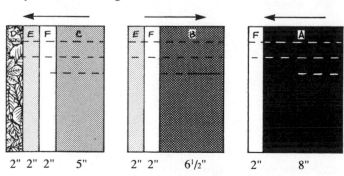

2" 2" 2" 5"   2" 2" 6½"   2" 8"

Strip size before sewing

Each of these units should measure 9½" from raw edge to raw edge. Arrows indicate in which direction strips should be pressed.

2. Place rows 1 and 2 together, rows 3 and 4 together, and rows 5 and 6 together. You will find seam allowances going in opposite directions! Cut every 2". You will need 48 cuts.

3. Sew into pairs, then join pairs. Make 48 blocks that look like this:

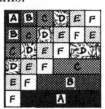

Press all seams toward row 6. These blocks should measure 9½" from raw edge to raw edge.

4. Sew 4 of these blocks to make a major block that looks like this:

Make 12.

5. Following illustration, sew blocks into rows.

Border and Finishing
1. After pieced area is completed, add border. Piece the 3½" strips of border fabric on the slant and measure off 2 strips, each 54½" long. Sew to top and bottom; press. Measure off 2 strips, each 78½" long, and sew to long sides. Press.

2. Layer, quilt, and bind.

The addition of a pieced border adds great interest to this simple quilt. The pieced border uses the featured unit, which is discussed on page 5.

Fabric A

Fabric B

Fabric C

Fabric D

Fabric E

Fabric F

Large Quilt

Block size: 18"
Number of blocks: 20 blocks, set 4 by 5
Pieced area finishes to 72" x 90".
After first border, quilt will be 76$\frac{1}{2}$" x 93$\frac{1}{2}$".
After pieced border, quilt will be 85" x 102".
After last border, quilt will be 90" x 107".

FABRIC REQUIREMENTS

45" wide fabric (see page 5)

Fabric A (darkest): 2¼ yds. (1¼ yds. for piecing, 1 yd. for pieced border)

Fabric B (darker): 4¼ yds. (1½ yds. for piecing, 1¾ yds. for first and last borders, 1 yd. for pieced border)

Fabric C (dark): 1½ yds.

Fabric D (light): 1½ yds.

Fabric E (lighter): 1½ yds.

Fabric F (lightest): 2½ yds. (1½ yds. for piecing, 1 yd. for pieced border)

Backing: 9½ yds.

Binding: 1 yd.

CUTTING REQUIREMENTS

Fabric A (Darkest)

1. Cut 4 strips 8" wide.
2. Cut 4 strips 2" wide.

For pieced border:

Cut 8 strips 3½" wide. Cut into 84 squares 3½".

Fabric B (Darker)

1. Cut 4 strips 6½" wide.
2. Cut 8 strips 2" wide.
3. Cut 4 strips 2¼" wide for first border.
4. Cut 6 strips 2¾" wide for first border.
5. Cut 11 strips 3" wide for last border.

For pieced border:

Cut 9 strips 2" wide. Cut into 168 squares 2".

Fabric C (Dark)

1. Cut 4 strips 5" wide.
2. Cut 12 strips 2" wide.

Fabric D (Light)

1. Cut 4 strips 3½" wide.
2. Cut 16 strips 2" wide.

Fabric E (Lighter)

Cut 24 strips 2" wide.

Fabric F (Lightest)

Cut 24 strips 2" wide.

For pieced border:

1. Cut 8 strips 3⅜" wide. Cut into 82 squares 3⅜". Cut these with an X to yield 328 quarter-square triangles.

2. Cut 2 squares 3". Cut these once diagonally to yield 4 half-square triangles for the corners.

Binding

Cut 11 strips 2½" wide.

PIECING AND ASSEMBLY

Blocks

1. Make 4 each of the following set-ups:

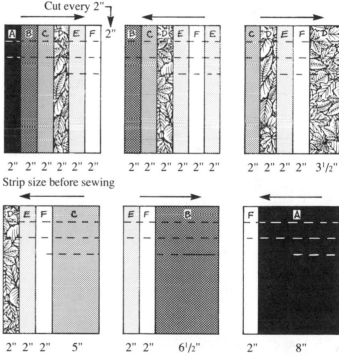

Each of these set-ups should measure 9½" from raw edge to raw edge. Arrows indicate direction in which seams should be pressed.

2. Place rows 1 and 2 right sides together, rows 3 and 4 right sides together, and rows 5 and 6 right sides together. You will find seam allowances going in opposite directions! Cut every 2". You will need 80 cuts.

3. Sew rows together into blocks that look like this:

Make 80

Press all seams toward row 6. These blocks should measure 9½" from raw edge to raw edge.
4. Sew 4 of these together to make a major block that looks like this:

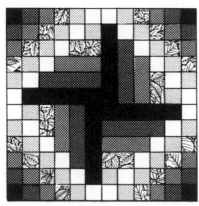
Make 20

Make 20 blocks.
5. Following illustration on page 10, sew in rows.

Borders and Finishing

1. After pieced area is complete, add first border. Piece the 2¼" wide strips of Fabric B on the slant and measure off 2 strips, each 72½" long. Sew to top and bottom; press. Piece the 2¾" wide strips of Fabric B on the slant and measure off 2 strips, each 94" long. Sew to long sides; press.
2. Add pieced and last borders, if desired (see CREATIVE OPTION); layer, quilt, and bind.

CREATIVE OPTION

After the first border, you may add a pieced border.

1. Make 160 units that look like this:

Make 160

Hint: When sewing the small triangles onto squares, place triangles under squares to keep bias edges from stretching.
2. Make 72 units that look like this:

Make 72

3. Make 4 units for right sides of border strips that look like this:

Make 4

4. Make 4 units for left sides of border strips that look like this:

Make 4

5. Make 4 corner units that look like this:

Make 4

6. Sew 2 border strips of 16 units each, then add a right end unit and a left end unit. Sew to top and bottom, starting and stopping your stitching ¼" from the ends. Press.
7. Sew 2 border strips of 20 units each, then add a right end unit and a left end unit. Sew to long sides, starting and stopping your stitching ¼" from the ends. Press.
8. Close up seams on squares.
9. Add corner units.
10. Piece the 3" wide strips of Fabric B on the slant for the last border. Measure off 2 strips, each 85½" long, and sew to top and bottom. Press. Measure off 2 strips, each 107½" long, and sew to long sides. Press.

DAVID AND GOLIATH

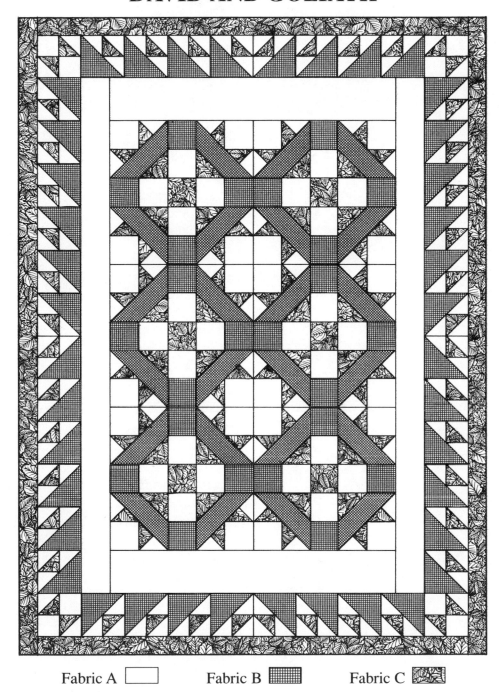

Fabric A ☐   Fabric B ▦   Fabric C ▨

The 10" block used in this quilt can be found in many quilt books and has a variety of different names. In this version, I used the same pieced block throughout, then added a striking pieced border.

Lesson: Handling quarter-square triangles. The pieced border repeats the featured unit, which is described on page 5.

Wall Hanging

Block size: 10"
Number of blocks: 6
Pieced area finishes to 20" x 30".
After first border, quilt will be 24" x 36".
After pieced border, quilt will be 30" x 42".
After last border, quilt will be 33" x 45".

FABRIC REQUIREMENTS

45" wide fabric (see page 5)
Fabric A (background): 2 yds. (½ yd. for piecing, ¾ yd. for pieced border, ¾ yd. for first and last borders)
Fabric B (main): ⅞ yd. (½ yd. for piecing, ⅜ yd. for pieced border)
Fabric C (accent): ¾ yd. (⅜ yd. for piecing, ⅜ yd. for pieced border)
Backing: 1½ yds.
Binding: ½ yd.

CUTTING INSTRUCTIONS

Fabric A (background)

1. Cut 2 strips 2½" wide. Cut into 24 squares 2½".
2. Cut 2 strips 2½" wide.
3. Cut 1 strip 3¼" wide. Cut into 12 squares 3¼". Cut these with an X to yield 48 quarter-square triangles.

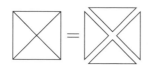

4. Cut 2 strips 2½" wide and 2 strips 3½" wide for first border.
5. Cut 5 strips 2" wide for last border.

For pieced border:
1. Cut 3 strips 2⅜" wide. Cut into 40 squares 2⅜". Cut these once diagonally to yield 80 half-square triangles.

2. Cut 1 strip 2" wide. Cut into 8 squares 2".
3. Using ⅜ yd., mark a 2⅜" grid of 4 squares by 6 squares to be sewn with Fabric C (accent). Following illustration, draw diagonal lines.

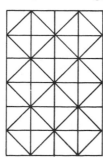

Fabric B (main)

1. Cut 2 strips 2½" wide.
2. Cut 4 strips 1⅞" wide. Cut into 24 "decapitated triangles," by measuring 45° cuts at 6⅞". (See page 96 for more information on cutting "decapitated triangles.")

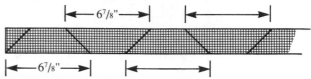

For pieced border:
    Cut 2 strips 3⅞" wide. Cut into 20 squares 3⅞". Cut these once diagonally to yield 40 half-square triangles.

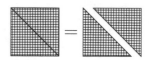

Fabric C (accent)

1. Cut 1 strip 3¼" wide. Cut into 12 squares 3¼". Cut these squares with an X to yield 48 quarter-square triangles.

2. Cut 1 strip 2⅞" wide. Cut into 12 squares 2⅞". Cut these once diagonally to yield 24 half-square triangles.

3. Cut 1 strip 2½" wide. Cut into 6 squares 2½".

For pieced border:
    Set aside ⅜ yd. to be sewn with Fabric A (background) for fast triangles.

Binding
Cut 5 strips 2" wide.

PIECING AND ASSEMBLY

Blocks
1. With the 2½" wide strips of fabrics A and B

(background and main), sew 2 sets of strips that look like this:

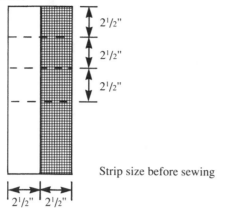

Strip size before sewing

Cut every 2½". You will need 24 cuts.

2. To make quarter-square units, sew 24 pairs with Fabric A (background) on top:

These units will end up looking like this:

 Make 24

Sew 24 pairs with Fabric C (accent) on top:

These units will end up looking like this:

 Make 24

3. Add these units to the Fabric A (background) squares:

Add these units and Fabric C (accent) triangles to the "decapitated triangles":

 Make 24

4. Sew in rows to make blocks:

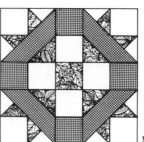 Make 6

5. Following illustration on page 13, sew 6 blocks together.

Borders and Finishing

1. After piecing is completed, add first border. With the 3½" wide Fabric A (background) strips, measure off 2 strips, each 20½" long. Sew to top and bottom; press. With the 2½" wide Fabric A (background) strips, measure off 2 strips, each 36½" long. Sew to long sides; press.

2. Add pieced and last borders, if desired (see CREATIVE OPTION); layer, quilt, and bind.

CREATIVE OPTION

After adding the first border, a pieced border may be added.

1. With fabrics A and C (background and accent) right sides together, mark a 2⅜" grid of squares:

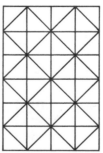

Sew ¼" seam on each side of the drawn diagonal lines.

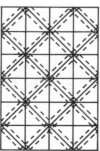

Cut apart and press open. These should measure 2" from raw edge to raw edge. You will need 48 of these half-square triangles.

Make 48

|←2"→|

2. Sew a triangle onto each side of 40 triangle units (the featured unit).

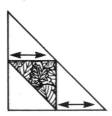

3. Add these units to the Fabric B (main) half-square triangles:

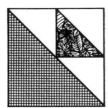

4. Make 4 corner units that look like this:

5. Sew 2 border strips, each with 8 units. Reverse units in the middle so you have 4 going 1 direction and 4 going the other direction. They should look like this:

Sew to top and bottom; press.

6. Sew 2 border strips, each with 12 units. Reverse units in the middle so you have 6 units going 1 direction and 6 going the other direction. Sew a corner unit onto each end.

Sew to long sides; press.

7. With the 2" wide strips of Fabric A (background), measure off 2 strips, each 30$\frac{1}{2}$" long, and sew to top and bottom. Press. Piece the remaining strips and measure off 2 strips, each 45$\frac{1}{2}$" long, and sew to long sides. Press.

CALIFORNIA STAR

Fabric A ▢   Fabric B ▮

When I saw this Feathered Star design on an antique quilt, I was immediately attracted to it. I realized that it would adapt well to rotary cutting, since all the shapes are regular sizes. I especially liked the large center in which a number of pieced designs could be used. The California Star quilt features the Ohio Star, while the California Twist features an 18" Around the Twist design. Although the number and size of the feathers on the sides of the star points vary more than most California Star designs, I liked the design enough to use it.

Lesson: Making small pieced blocks and fast triangles, using quarter-square triangles.

Wall Hanging

Number of blocks: Overall design
Pieced area finishes to 38" square.
After border, quilt will be 43" square.

Note: It is necessary to use $1/16$" measurements in these patterns for accuracy. Don't panic: It's only $1/2$ of an $1/8$". It looks like this:

$1/16$"

This small amount compounded over 6 pieces is over $1/3$", so be sure to measure accurately.

FABRIC REQUIREMENTS

45" wide fabric (see page 5)
Fabric A (background): 2 yds.
Fabric B (main): $2^1/8$ yds. (1 yd. for piecing, $5/8$ yd.
  for border, $1/2$ yd. for binding)
Backing: $2^3/4$ yds.

CUTTING INSTRUCTIONS

Fabric A (background)
For center section:
1. Cut 2 strips $2^1/2$" wide. Cut into 20 squares $2^1/2$".
2. Cut 1 strip $3^1/4$" wide. Cut into 10 squares $3^1/4$".
   Cut these with an X to yield 40 quarter-square
   triangles.

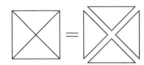

For Feathered Stars:
1. Cut 1 square $19^1/4$". Cut with an X to yield 4
   quarter-square triangles.
2. Cut 2 strips $10^1/2$" wide. Cut into 4 squares
   $10^1/2$".
3. Cut 1 strip $2^5/16$" wide. Cut into 4 squares $2^5/16$".
   Cut these once diagonally to yield 8 half-square
   triangles.

4. Mark a $2^7/8$" grid of 16 squares for large fast
   triangles. Draw the diagonal lines, following
   illustration.

$2^7/8$" grid

Mark a $2^5/16$" grid of 24 squares for small fast
triangles. Following illustration, draw the diagonal lines.

$2^5/16$" grid

Fabric B (main)
For center section:
1. Cut 1 strip $6^1/2$" wide. Cut into 4 squares $6^1/2$".

2. Cut 1 strip $2^1/2$" wide. Cut into 5 squares $2^1/2$".
3. Cut 1 strip $3^1/4$" wide. Cut into 10 squares $3^1/4$".
   Cut these with an X to yield 40 quarter-square
   triangles.

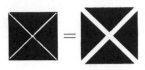

For Feathered Stars:
1. Set aside $1/2$ yd. to go with Fabric A (background) for fast triangles.
2. Cut 4 squares $2^7/8$". Cut these once diagonally to
   yield 8 half-square triangles for feather points.

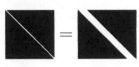

3. Cut 2 squares $2^5/16$". Cut these once diagonally
   to yield 4 half-square triangles.

4. Cut 1 strip $6^7/8$" wide. Cut into 4 squares $6^7/8$".
   Cut these once diagonally to yield 8 half-square
   triangles.

For borders and binding:
1. Cut 5 strips 3" wide for border.
2. Cut 5 strips $2^1/2$" wide for binding.

PIECING AND ASSEMBLY

Center Section
1. With Fabric A (background) quarter-square
   triangles on top of Fabric B (main) quarter-
   square triangles, sew 40 pairs.

Join into squares.

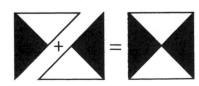

2. Make 5 Ohio Star blocks:

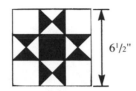

These blocks should measure 6½" from raw edge to raw edge.

3. Make large center block, alternating Ohio Star blocks and plain squares of Fabric B (main). This large block should measure 18½" from raw edge to raw edge.

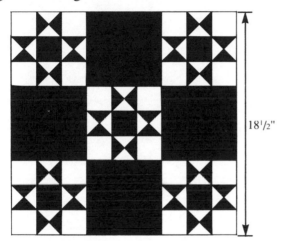

Feathered Stars

1. Placing gridded Fabric A (background) right sides together with reserved ½ yd. of Fabric B (main), sew a ¼" seam on each side of the drawn diagonal lines. Cut apart and press.

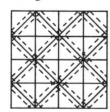

The large triangle units should measure 2½" from raw edge to raw edge; the small triangles should measure 1¹⁵/₁₆" from raw edge to raw edge.

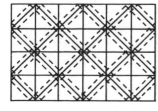

2. Sew 6 small triangle units together. Sew 4 strips going 1 direction

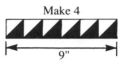

and 4 strips going the other direction.

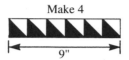

These strips should measure 9" from raw edge to raw edge.

3. Add a small Fabric A (background) triangle to the end of each strip to look like this:

Sew these units to long side of large triangles.

4. Sew 4 large triangle units together. Sew 4 strips heading 1 direction and 4 strips going the opposite direction.

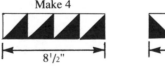

These strips should measure 8½" from raw edge to raw edge.

5. Following illustration on page 17, add large triangle strips to short sides of large triangles.
   Make 4 that look like this:

Make 4

and 4 that look like this:

Make 4

6. Sew a Fabric B (main) 2⅞" triangle to the end.

7. Add 1 of these triangle units to large background
   triangle. Add a small triangle to the other triangle unit; join to background triangle.

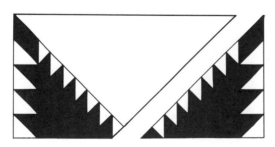

Add triangle

8. Sew 1 of these units to each side of the pieced
   center section.

9. Onto each side of the remaining 2 units, sew a
   background square:

10. Sew these 3 rows together.

Border and Finishing
1. After pieced area is completed, add border. With
   the 3" wide strips of Fabric B (main), measure
   off 2 strips, each 38½" long, and sew to 2
   opposite sides. Press. Piece the remaining 3"
   strips (on the slant). Measure off 2 strips, each
   43½" long, and sew to other sides. Press.
2. Layer, quilt, and bind.

CALIFORNIA TWIST

In this variation, the center is a 17" miniature Around the Twist, with a ½" border to build it up to the required 18". You could easily substitute other 18" blocks as well.

Fabric A
Fabric B
Fabric C

Wall Hanging

Number of blocks: Overall design
Pieced area finishes to 38" square.
After first border, quilt will be 45³/₄" square.
After pieced border, quilt will be 53" square.
After last border, quilt will be 57" square.

FABRIC REQUIREMENTS

45" wide fabric (see page 5)
Fabric A (background): 2½ yds. (2 yds. for piecing, ½ yd. for pieced border)
Fabric B (feather): 1⅓ yds. (1 yd. for piecing, ⅓ yd. for pieced border)
Fabric C (accent): 2½ yds. (½ yd. for piecing, ¾ yd. for pieced border, 1¼ yds. for first and last borders)
Backing: 3½ yds.
Binding: ½ yd.

CUTTING INSTRUCTIONS

Fabric A (background)

For center section:
1. Cut 2 strips 3½" wide. Cut into 16 squares 3½". Using the 1" Speedy on the Rotary Mate™, cut 2 corners off each of 4 squares, 3 corners off each of 8 squares, and all 4 corners off each of 4 squares to make Snowball blocks.

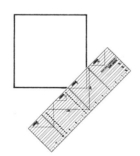

  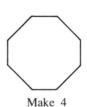

Make 4   Make 8   Make 4

2. Cut 1 strip 5½" wide. Cut into 3 squares 5½". Cut these with an X to yield 12 quarter-square triangles. It would be helpful to notch these triangles at 3½".

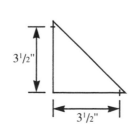

3. Cut 1 strip 1½" wide. Cut into 9 squares 1½".

For Feathered Stars:
1. Cut 1 square 19¼". Cut with an X to yield 4 quarter-square triangles.

2. Cut 2 strips 10½" wide. Cut into 4 squares 10½".
3. Cut 1 strip 2⁵/₁₆" wide. Cut into 4 squares 2⁵/₁₆". Cut these once diagonally to yield 8 half-square triangles.

4. Mark a 2⅞" grid of 16 squares for large fast triangles. Following illustration, mark the diagonal lines.

Mark a 2⁵/₁₆" grid of 24 squares for small fast triangles. Following illustration, mark the diagonal lines.

For pieced border:
1. Cut 4 strips 2⁵/₈" wide. Cut into 52 squares 2⁵/₈".

Fabric B (feather)

For center section:
1. Cut 1 strip 2½" wide. Cut into 18 rectangles 1½" x 2½".
2. Cut 1 strip 1⅞" wide. Cut into 12 squares 1⅞". Cut these once diagonally to yield 24 half-square triangles.

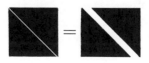

For Feathered Stars:
1. Set aside ½ yd. to go with Fabric A (background) for fast triangles.
2. Cut 4 squares 2⅞". Cut these once diagonally to yield 8 half-square triangles for the feather points.

3. Cut 2 squares 2⁵/₁₆". Cut these once diagonally to yield 4 half-square triangles.

For pieced border:
Cut 4 strips 2" wide. With strips folded in half, cut into 56 diamonds. (See page 96 for more information on cutting diamonds.) Make bias cuts every 2", lining up 45° angle on ruler like this:

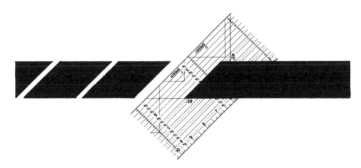

Fabric C (accent)

For center section:
1. Cut 2 squares 3" wide. Cut these once diagonally to yield 4 corner triangles.

2. Cut 1 strip 2½" wide. Cut into 18 rectangles 1½" x 2½".
3. Cut 1 strip 1⅞" wide. Cut into 12 squares 1⅞". Cut these once diagonally to yield 24 half-square triangles.

4. Cut 2 strips 1" wide for narrow border on center section.

For Feathered Stars:
Cut 1 strip 6⅞" wide. Cut into 4 squares 6⅞". Cut these once diagonally to yield 8 half-square triangles.

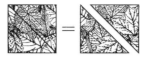

For first and last borders:
1. Cut 5 strips 4⅜" wide for first border.
2. Cut 6 strips 2½" wide for last border.

For pieced border:
1. Cut 5 strips 2" wide. With strips folded in half, cut into 48 trapezoids, cutting back at 4½". (See page 95 for more information on cutting trapezoids.)

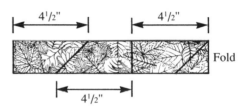

You will need 24 that look like this:

and 24 that look like this:

2. Cut 2 strips 2⅜" wide. Cut into 28 squares 2⅜". Cut these once diagonally to yield 56 half-square triangles.

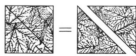

3. Cut 4 squares 2⅝".
4. Cut 4 rectangles 2" x 2⅝" for extra end units.

Binding
Cut 6 strips 2½" wide.

PIECING AND ASSEMBLY

Note: This Around the Twist finishes to 17". If you add ½" borders, the block will be the proper size (18").

Center Section

1. Starting with the small Fabric A (background) square on top of Fabric B (feather) rectangle, stitch halfway down the square and stop.

Working in a circle, sew the rectangles onto the center, alternating Fabric C (accent) and Fabric B (feather). Then close up the opening.

   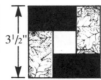

3½"

Make 9

Make 9 blocks.

2. Following illustration on page 21, sew appropriate Fabric C (accent) and Fabric B (feather) triangles onto Fabric A (background) Snowball blocks.

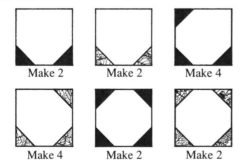

Make 2   Make 2   Make 4

Make 4   Make 2   Make 2

3. Starting in a corner, join in rows. Add setting triangles onto ends of rows, matching notches to ends of blocks.

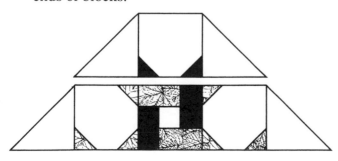

4. After rows are joined, add corners.
5. From the 1" strips of Fabric C (accent), cut 2 lengths 17½" and 2 lengths 18½". Sew the 17½" lengths to the top and bottom of center section. Press. Sew the 18½" lengths to the sides. Press.

Feathered Stars

Follow instructions on pages 19–20, steps 1–10, to make star points.

Borders and Finishing

1. When star is completed, add first border. With the 4⅜" strips of Fabric C (accent), measure off 2 strips, each 38½" long, and sew to 2 opposite sides. Press. Piece the remaining strips on the slant and measure off 2 strips, each 46¼" long. Sew to the other sides. Press.
2. Add the pieced and last borders, if desired (see CREATIVE OPTION); layer, quilt, and bind.

CREATIVE OPTION

After the first border, you may add a pieced border. This pieced border is really made from attic window units. However, instead of using two trapezoids, only one trapezoid is used and the other is subcut into a diamond and a triangle. Two mirror-image blocks are alternated.

1. Make 24 A units that look like this:

Make 24

and 24 B units that look like this:

Make 24

2. Make 4 end units that look like this:

Make 4

3. Make 4 corner units that look like this:

Make 4

4. Sew 4 strips, each with 12 units, alternating A and B units.

 Make 4

5. Add an end unit to one end of each border strip.

6. Sew 2 of these border strips to opposite sides of quilt. Press.
7. Onto each end of the remaining strips, add a corner unit. Sew to quilt; press.

8. Piece the 2½" strips of Fabric C (accent) on the slant and measure off 2 strips, each 53½" long. Sew to 2 opposite sides. Press. Measure off 2 strips, each 57½" long, and sew to remaining sides. Press.

STAR IN HEAVEN

In this quilt, I used a 12" block, known as June Bride. This block first appeared in Judy Martin's *Ultimate Book of Quilt Block Patterns*. The alternate block is a larger Puss-in-the-Corner block repeated from the pieced border. This setting should allow you to substitute any 12" block for the June Bride block, if you wish.

Lesson: Piecing setting triangles, flying geese units, attic window units; cutting trapezoids; strip piecing; making diagonally set quilt.

Lap Quilt

Block size: 12"
Number of blocks: 18 (12 star blocks and 6 alternate blocks)
Pieced area finishes to $56\frac{5}{8}$" x $73\frac{5}{8}$".
After border, quilt will be $64\frac{5}{8}$" x $81\frac{5}{8}$".

Fabric A
Fabric B
Fabric C
Fabric D

FABRIC REQUIREMENTS

45" wide fabric (see page 5)
Fabric A: 2 yds.
Fabric B: 1⁷/₈ yds. (1 yd. for piecing, ⁷/₈ yd. for border)
Fabric C: 2¹/₄ yds.
Fabric D: 1¹/₄ yds.
Backing: 5 yds.
Binding: ³/₄ yd.

CUTTING INSTRUCTIONS

Fabric A

1. Cut 5 strips 3¹/₂" wide into 48 squares 3¹/₂" for pieced blocks.
2. Cut 3 strips 7¹/₄" wide into 12 squares 7¹/₄". Cut these with an **X** to yield 48 quarter-square triangles for pieced blocks.

3. Cut 2 strips 2¹/₂" wide for Four Patches in setting triangles.
4. Cut 3 strips 6⁷/₈" wide into 11 squares 6⁷/₈". Cut these with an **X** to yield 42 setting triangles.

5. Cut 2 squares 3³/₄". Cut these once diagonally to yield the 4 corners.

Fabric B

1. Cut 2 strips 4³/₄" wide. Cut into 12 squares 4³/₄" for pieced blocks.
2. Cut 3 strips 2" wide. Cut into 48 squares 2" for pieced blocks.
3. Cut 1 strip 3¹/₂" wide for large Puss-in-the-Corner blocks.
4. Cut 2 strips 2" wide for large Puss-in-the-Corner blocks.
5. Cut 2 strips 2¹/₂" wide for small Puss-in-the-Corner blocks.
6. Cut 2 strips 1¹/₂" wide for small Puss-in-the-Corner blocks.
7. Cut 8 strips 4¹/₂" wide for border.

Fabric C

1. Cut 8 strips 2" wide. With strips folded in half, cut 96 trapezoids at 3⁷/₈" intervals, beginning measurement along top edge. These will be for the pieced blocks.

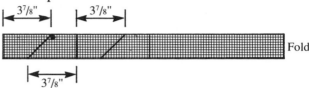

You will need 48 going 1 direction and 48 reversed.

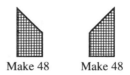

Make 48   Make 48

2. Cut 3 strips 2" wide for small Four Patches.
3. Cut 4 strips 3¹/₂" wide. Cut every 6¹/₂". You will need 24 cuts.
4. Cut 5 strips 4¹/₂" wide. Cut 20 trapezoids at 8⁷/₈" intervals, beginning measurement along top edge.

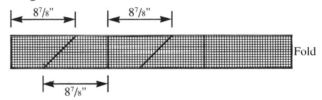

You will need 10 going in 1 direction and 10 reversed.

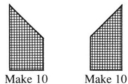

Make 10   Make 10

5. Cut 1 strip 2¹/₂" wide for small Puss-in-the-Corner blocks.
6. Cut 1 strip 3¹/₂" wide for large Puss-in-the-Corner blocks.
7. Cut 2 strips 2¹/₂" wide for large Four Patches.
8. Cut 1 strip 4¹/₂" wide. Cut into 4 squares 4¹/₂" for corner sections.

Fabric D

1. Cut 4 strips 3" wide. Cut into 48 squares 3". Cut these once diagonally to yield 96 half-square triangles for pieced blocks.

2. Cut 4 strips 2½" wide for large Four Patches.
3. Cut 4 strips 1½" wide for small Puss-in-the-Corner blocks.
4. Cut 2 strips 2" wide for large Puss-in-the-Corner blocks.
5. Cut 3 strips 2" wide for small Four Patches.

Binding

Cut 8 strips 2½" wide.

PIECING AND ASSEMBLY

Star Blocks

1. Sew a trapezoid onto 1 side of 3½" squares of Fabric A (background).

2. Add a small square of Fabric B onto the end of an opposite trapezoid and add to other side:

3. Add a triangle of Fabric D to each side of this unit.

4. Add 1 of these units onto each side of center square.

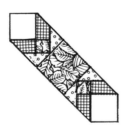

5. Onto 2 units, add a large quarter-square triangle of Fabric A (background) to each side.

6. Make 12 blocks. These should measure 12½" from raw edge to raw edge.

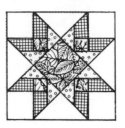

Puss-in-the-Corner Blocks

1. Make 1 set of strips that looks like this:

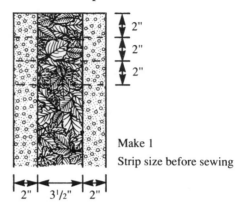

Make 1

Strip size before sewing

2"   3½"   2"

Make cuts at 2"; you will need 12 cuts.

2. Make 1 set of strips that looks like this:

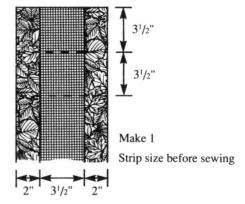

Make 1

Strip size before sewing

2"   3½"   2"

Make cuts at 3½"; you will need 6 cuts.

3. Make 6 large Puss-in-the-Corner blocks:

Make 6

4. Make 3 sets of strips that look like this:

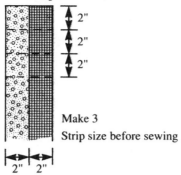

Make 3
Strip size before sewing

Place 2 strips right sides together and cut every 2". You will need 24 cuts. Make 24 Four Patches.

5. Make 6 larger Puss-in-the-Corner blocks:

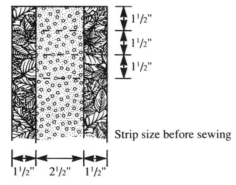

Make 6

Setting Triangles

1. Make 2 sets of strips that looks like this:

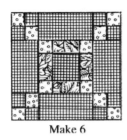

Strip size before sewing

Make cuts at $1\frac{1}{2}$"; you will need 28 cuts.

2. Make 1 set of strips that look like this:

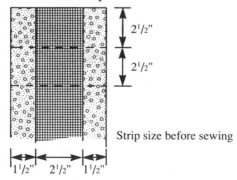

Strip size before sewing

Make cuts at $2\frac{1}{2}$"; you will need 14 cuts.

3. Make 14 small Puss-in-the-Corner blocks:

Make 14

4. Make 2 sets of strips that look like this:

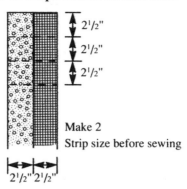

Make 2
Strip size before sewing

and 2 sets of strips that look like this:

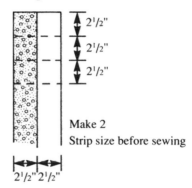

Make 2
Strip size before sewing

Place these 2 rows right sides together and cut every $2\frac{1}{2}$". You will need 28 cuts. Sew in pairs.

5. Make 28 Four Patches.

Make 28

6. Make 3 setting triangle units that look like this:

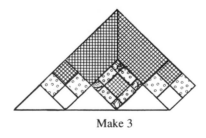

Make 3

Make 3 setting triangle units that look like this:

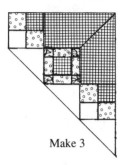

Make 3

Make 4 setting triangle units that look like this:

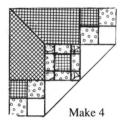

Make 4

Make 4 corner units:

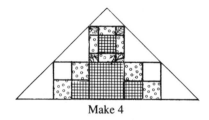

Make 4

7. Starting in a corner and following illustration on page 26, assemble in rows. Add corners last.

Border and Finishing

1. After piecing is completed, add border. Piece the 4$\frac{1}{2}$" wide strips of Fabric B on the slant and measure off 2 strips, each 57$\frac{1}{8}$" long, and sew to top and bottom. Press. Measure off 2 strips, each 82$\frac{1}{8}$" long, and sew to long sides. Press.
2. Layer, quilt, and bind.

Large Quilt

Block size: 12"

Number of blocks: 32 (20 star blocks and 12 alternate blocks)

Pieced area finishes to 73$\frac{1}{2}$" x 90$\frac{1}{2}$".

After first border, quilt will be 77" x 94".

After last border, quilt will be 84" x 101".

Fabric A
Fabric B
Fabric C
Fabric D

FABRIC REQUIREMENTS

45" wide fabric (see page 5)
Fabric A: $4\frac{1}{2}$ yds.
Fabric B: $3\frac{1}{2}$ yds. (2 yds. for piecing, $1\frac{1}{2}$ yds. for last border)
Fabric C: $2\frac{1}{2}$ yds. ($1\frac{3}{4}$ yds. for piecing, $\frac{3}{4}$ yd. for first border)
Fabric D: $\frac{3}{4}$ yd.
Backing: 9 yds.
Binding: 1 yd.

CUTTING INSTRUCTIONS

Fabric A

1. Cut 4 strips $7\frac{1}{4}$" wide. Cut these into 20 squares $7\frac{1}{4}$"; then cut these with an X to yield 80 quarter-square triangles.

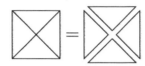

2. Cut 3 strips $4\frac{1}{4}$" wide. Cut these into 20 squares $4\frac{1}{4}$"; then cut these with an X to yield 80 quarter-square triangles.

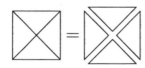

3. Cut 4 strips 2" wide. Cut into 80 squares 2".
4. Cut 8 strips $3\frac{1}{2}$" wide. Cut into 80 squares $3\frac{1}{2}$".
5. Cut 1 strip $3\frac{1}{2}$" wide for large Puss-in-the-Corner blocks.
6. Cut 5 strips $6\frac{1}{2}$" wide. Cut every $3\frac{1}{2}$" to yield 48 rectangles.
7. Cut 6 strips 2" wide for small Four Patches.
8. Cut 5 strips $4\frac{1}{2}$" wide. With strips folded in half, cut 28 trapezoids at $8\frac{7}{8}$" intervals, beginning measurement along top edge. (See page 95 for more information on cutting trapezoids.)

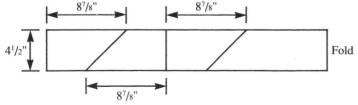

You will need 14 that look like this:

and 14 that look like this:

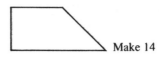

9. Cut 1 strip $4\frac{1}{2}$" wide. Cut into 4 squares $4\frac{1}{2}$".
10. Cut 3 strips $2\frac{1}{2}$" wide for large Four Patches.

Fabric B

1. Cut 6 strips $2\frac{1}{2}$" wide for Four Patches.
2. Cut 8 strips $3\frac{7}{8}$" wide. Cut into 80 squares $3\frac{7}{8}$". Cut these diagonally to yield 160 half-square triangles.

3. Cut 2 strips $2\frac{1}{2}$" wide for small Puss-in-the-Corner blocks.
4. Cut 4 strips $1\frac{1}{2}$" wide for small Puss-in-the-Corner blocks.
5. Cut 2 strips $3\frac{1}{2}$" wide for center of star blocks. Cut into 20 squares $3\frac{1}{2}$".
6. Cut 10 strips 4" wide for last border.

Fabric C

1. Cut 5 strips $2\frac{3}{8}$" wide. Cut into 80 squares $2\frac{3}{8}$". Cut these once diagonally to yield 160 half-square triangles.

2. Cut 3 strips $2\frac{1}{2}$" wide for large Four Patches.
3. Cut 3 strips $6\frac{7}{8}$" wide into 14 squares $6\frac{7}{8}$". Cut these with an X to yield 54 setting triangles.

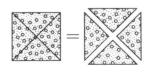

4. Cut 2 squares $3\frac{3}{4}$". Cut these once diagonally to yield the 4 corners.

5. Cut 6 strips 2" wide for small Four Patches.
6. Cut 4 strips 2" wide for large Puss-in-the-Corner blocks.
7. Cut 9 strips 2¼" wide for first border.

Fabric D

1. Cut 2 strips 2½" wide for small Puss-in-the-Corner blocks.
2. Cut 2 strips 2" wide for large Puss-in-the-Corner blocks.
3. Cut 4 strips 1½" wide for small Puss-in-the-Corner blocks.
4. Cut 2 strips 3½" wide for large Puss-in-the-Corner blocks.

Binding

Cut 10 strips 2½" wide.

PIECING AND ASSEMBLY

Note: This quilt is easier to assemble if you make all your basic units first.

Star Blocks

1. The Rising Star block is an Evening Star block inside another Evening Star. Assemble the small stars first. Make 80 small flying geese units:

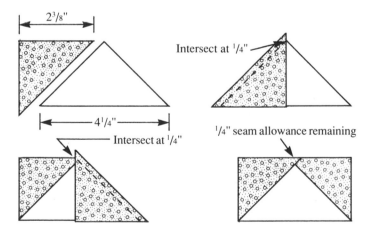

Hint: Sew 1 side on first, lining it up at pointed end and making sure it intersects at ¼". Press; then add second triangle. When sewing on second triangle, be sure that top point intersects at ¼". This will result in a straight edge at the top, with the correct seam allowance remaining.

2. Join in rows to make 20 small Evening Star blocks:

Make 20

3. Make the large star, using the small star as the center block. Make 80 large flying geese units.

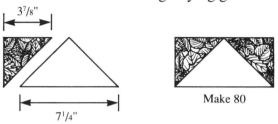

Make 80

4. Join in rows to make 20 large Evening Star blocks.

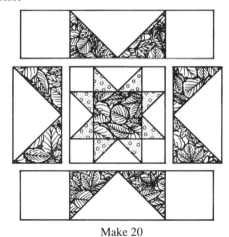

Make 20

These blocks should measure 12½" from raw edge to raw edge.

Puss-in-the-Corner Blocks (large)

1. Make 2 sets of strips that look like this:

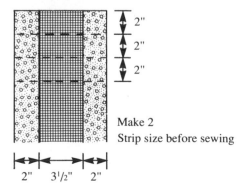

Make 2
Strip size before sewing

2" 3½" 2"

Make cuts at 2"; you will need 24 cuts.

2. Make 2 sets of strips that look like this:

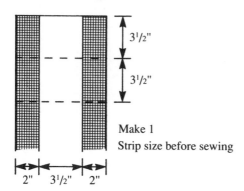

Make 1

Strip size before sewing

Make cuts at 3½"; you will need 12 cuts.

3. Make 12 large Puss-in-the-Corner blocks:

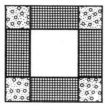

Make 12

4. To make Four Patches, make 6 sets of strips that look like this:

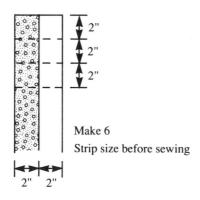

Make 6

Strip size before sewing

Place 2 strips right sides together and make cuts every 2". You will need 48 cuts. Sew in pairs to make 48 Four Patches.

Make 48

5. Add to Fabric A rectangles to make 12 large Puss-in-the-Corner blocks.

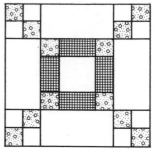

Make 12

Puss-in-the-Corner Blocks (small)

1. Make 2 sets of strips that look like this:

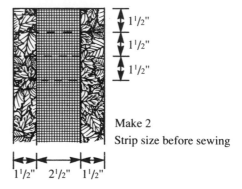

Make 2

Strip size before sewing

Make cuts at 1½"; you will need 36 cuts.

2. Make 2 sets of strips that look like this:

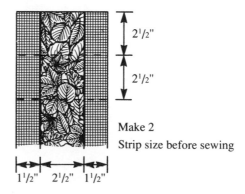

Make 2

Strip size before sewing

Make cuts at 2½"; you will need 18 cuts.

3. Make 18 blocks:

Make 18

Four Patches

1. Make 3 sets of strips that look like this:

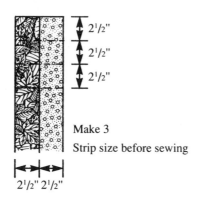

Make 3
Strip size before sewing

2¹/₂" 2¹/₂"

and 3 sets of strips that look like this:

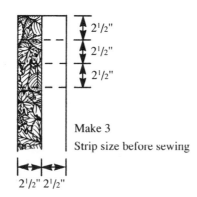

Make 3
Strip size before sewing

2¹/₂" 2¹/₂"

Place these 2 rows right sides together and cut every 2¹/₂". You will need 36 cuts. Sew in pairs.

Make 36

2. Make 4 corner units:

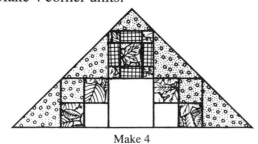

Make 4

3. Make 5 setting triangle units that look like this:

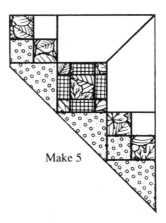

Make 5

and 5 setting triangle units that look like this:

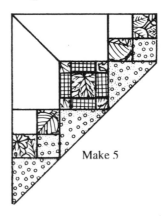

Make 5

Make 4 setting triangle units that look like this:

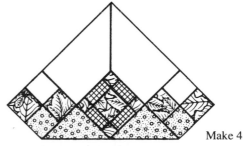

Make 4

4. Starting in a corner and following illustration on page 31, assemble in rows. Add corners last.

Borders and Finishing

1. After piecing is completed, add first border. Piece the 2¹/₄" wide strips of Fabric C on the slant and measure off 2 strips, each 74" long, and sew to top and bottom. Press. Measure off 2 strips, each 94¹/₂" long, and sew to long sides. Press.
2. Add second border. Piece the 4" wide strips of Fabric B on the slant and measure off 2 strips, each 77¹/₂" long, and sew to top and bottom. Press. Measure off 2 strips, each 101¹/₂" long, and sew to long sides. Press.
3. Layer, quilt, and bind.

SAWTOOTH FLOWER

This design was inspired by a photograph that Jean Reiley of Camillus, New York, shared with me. I found this block to be very versatile, yielding many setting layouts. Two of these layouts are given here.

Lesson: Making fast half-square triangles, cutting trapezoids, piecing diagonal sets and pieced border.

Fabric A
Fabric B
Fabric C
Fabric D

Twin Quilt

Block size: 7½"
Number of blocks: 64
Pieced area finishes to 53" x 85".
After first border and corners, quilt will be 56" x 88".
After second border, quilt will be 60" x 92".
After third border, quilt will be 64" x 96".
After pieced border, quilt will be 68" x 100".
After last border, quilt will be 74" x 106".

FABRIC REQUIREMENTS

45" wide fabric (see page 5)

Fabric A (background): $3^1/2$ yds. ($2^3/4$ yds. for piecing, $3/4$ yd. for pieced border)

Fabric B (main): $3^1/2$ yds. (2 yds. for piecing, $1^1/2$ yds. for second and last borders)

Fabric C (accent): $1^3/4$ yds. (1 yd. for piecing, $3/4$ yd. for first border)

Fabric D (stem): $3^1/4$ yds. ($1^3/4$ yds. for piecing, $3/4$ yd. for third border, $3/4$ yd. for pieced border)

Backing: $6^1/4$ yds.

Binding: 1 yd.

CUTTING INSTRUCTIONS

Fabric A (background)

1. Cut 11 strips 2" wide. With all strips right side up, cut 64 trapezoids at $6^7/8$" intervals, beginning measurement along bottom edge. (See page 95 for more information on cutting trapezoids.)

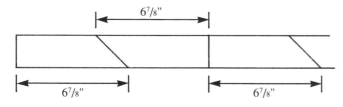

Trapezoids should look like this:

2. Cut 13 strips 2" wide. With all strips right side up, cut 64 trapezoids at $8^3/8$" intervals, beginning measurement along top edge.

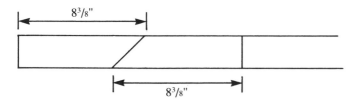

Trapezoids should look like this:

3. Cut 4 strips 2" wide. Cut into 64 squares 2".

4. With 1 yd. of fabric, mark a $2^3/8$" grid of squares. Working in sections, mark 128 squares. Following illustration, draw the diagonals.

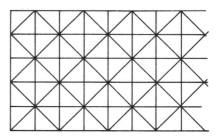

For pieced border:

1. Cut 4 squares $2^1/2$".
2. With $3/4$ yd. of fabric, mark a grid of $2^7/8$" squares for fast triangles. Working in sections, mark 80 squares. Following illustration, draw diagonals.

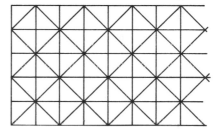

Fabric B (main)

1. Cut 6 strips $3^1/2$" wide. Cut into 64 squares $3^1/2$".
2. Cut 2 strips $11^7/8$" wide. Cut into 4 squares $11^7/8$". Cut with an **X** to yield 14 quarter-square triangles. It would be helpful to notch these at 8".

3. Cut 1 strip $17^5/8$" wide. Cut 2 squares $17^5/8$". Cut these once diagonally to yield the 4 corners. **Note:** The following border strips could be cut lengthwise instead of crosswise. Then you would need only 4 strips of each width.
4. Cut 7 strips $2^1/2$" wide for second border.
5. Cut 9 strips $3^1/2$" wide for last border.

Fabric C (accent)

1. Set aside 1 yd. to be sewn with Fabric A (background) for fast triangles.

2. Cut 8 strips 2" wide for first border.

Fabric D (stem)

1. Cut 4 strips 5" wide. Cut into 64 rectangles 2" x 5".
2. Cut 4 strips 6½" wide. Cut into 64 rectangles 2" x 6½".
3. Cut 4 strips 2⅜" wide. Cut into 64 squares 2⅜". Cut these once diagonally to yield 128 half-square triangles.

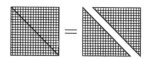

4. Cut 10 strips 2½" wide for third border.

For pieced border:

    Set aside ¾ yd. to be sewn with Fabric A (background) for fast triangles.

Binding

Cut 10 strips 2½" wide.

PIECING AND ASSEMBLY

Blocks

1. Place marked Fabric A (background) right sides together with Fabric C (accent) and sew a ¼" seam on each side of the diagonal lines.

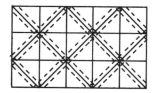

Cut apart and press. You will need 256 triangle units that measure 2" from raw edge to raw edge.

2. For each block, sew 2 triangle units going 1 direction and 2 triangles going the other direction:

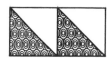 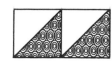

    Make 128   Make 128

Add 1 pair to the 3½" center block. Add a Fabric A (background) square to the other pair and add to center block:

3. Add the 5" and 6½" strips of Fabric D (stem) to block:

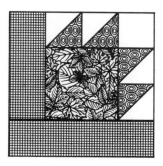

4. Sew triangle of Fabric D (stem) to end of trapezoids and add to block:

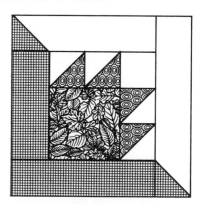

5. Assemble quilt in rows, adding setting triangles to ends of rows. Remember to match notches of setting triangles with ends of blocks.

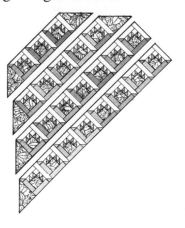

Borders and Finishing

1. With the 2" strips of Fabric C (accent), piece 4 strips on the slant and measure off 2 strips, each 53$\frac{1}{2}$" long. Sew to long sides. Cut 2 strips, each 21$\frac{3}{4}$" long, and sew to ends. Cut 4 strips, each 27$\frac{1}{4}$" long, and sew to corners. Trim.

2. Sew Fabric B (main) corners onto quilt.

3. Add second border. Piece the 2$\frac{1}{2}$" wide strips of Fabric B (main) and measure off 2 strips, each 56$\frac{1}{2}$" long, and sew to top and bottom. Press. Measure off 2 strips, each 92$\frac{1}{2}$" long, and sew to long sides. Press.

4. Add third border. Piece the 2$\frac{1}{2}$" wide strips of Fabric D (stem) and measure off 2 strips, each 60$\frac{1}{2}$" long, and sew to top and bottom. Press. Measure off 2 strips, each 96$\frac{1}{2}$" long, and sew to long sides. Press.

5. Add pieced and last borders, if desired (see CREATIVE OPTION); layer, quilt, and bind.

CREATIVE OPTION

After third border, a pieced border may be added. This border has a 2" repeat.

1. Make 160 triangle units. Place marked Fabric A (background) right sides together with Fabric D (stem) and stitch a $\frac{1}{4}$" seam on each side of diagonal lines.

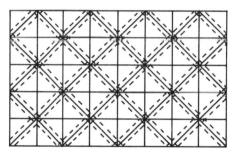

Cut apart and press. These units should measure 2$\frac{1}{2}$" from raw edge to raw edge.

2. Following quilt diagram on page 36, make 2 border strips of 32 units each, reversing in the middle. Sew to top and bottom. Press.

3. Following quilt diagram, make 2 border strips of 48 units, reversing in the middle. Add corner squares and sew to long sides. Press.

4. Piece the 3$\frac{1}{2}$" wide strips of Fabric B (main) and measure off 2 strips, each 68$\frac{1}{2}$" long. Sew to top and bottom. Press. Measure off 2 strips, each 106$\frac{1}{2}$" long, and sew to long sides. Press.

Large Quilt

Block size: 7$\frac{1}{2}$"
Number of blocks: 120 pieced blocks, set 10 by 12
Pieced area finishes to 75" x 90".
After first border, quilt will be 79" x 94".
After second border, quilt will be 85" x 100".

Fabric A
Fabric B
Fabric C
Fabric D

FABRIC REQUIREMENTS

45" wide fabric (see page 5)
Fabric A (background): 4$\frac{1}{2}$ yds.
Fabric B (main): 2$\frac{1}{4}$ yds. (1$\frac{1}{4}$ yds. for piecing, 1 yd.
   for second border)
Fabric C (accent): 2$\frac{1}{4}$ yds. (1$\frac{1}{4}$ yds. for piecing,
   $\frac{3}{4}$ yd. for first border)
Fabric D (stem): 2$\frac{3}{4}$ yds.
Backing: 9 yds.
Binding: 1 yd.

CUTTING INSTRUCTIONS

Fabric A (background)

1. Cut 20 strips 2" wide. With all strips right side up, cut 120 trapezoids at 6$\frac{7}{8}$" intervals, beginning measurement along bottom edge. (See page 95 for more information on cutting trapezoids.)

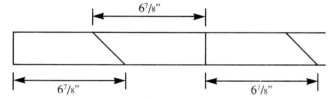

You will need 120 trapezoids with points going this way:

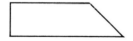

2. Cut 30 strips 2" wide. With all strips right side up, cut 120 trapezoids at 8$\frac{3}{8}$" intervals, beginning measurement along top edge.

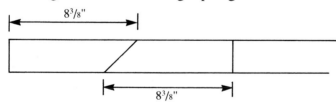

You will need 120 trapezoids with points going this way:

3. Cut 6 strips 2" wide. Cut into 120 squares 2".

4. With 1$\frac{1}{4}$ yds. of fabric, mark a 2$\frac{3}{8}$" grid of 240 squares. With this many squares, it is best to divide fabric into manageable sections. Following illustration, draw the diagonals.

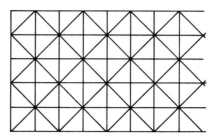

Fabric B (main)

1. Cut 11 strips 3$\frac{1}{2}$" wide. Cut into 120 squares 3$\frac{1}{2}$".
2. Cut 9 strips 3$\frac{1}{2}$" wide for last border.

Fabric C (accent)

1. Set aside 1$\frac{1}{4}$ yds. to be sewn with Fabric A (background) for fast triangles.
2. Cut 9 strips 2$\frac{1}{2}$" wide for first border.

Fabric D (stem)

1. Cut 6 strips 5" wide. Cut into 120 rectangles 2" x 5".
2. Cut 6 strips 6$\frac{1}{2}$" wide. Cut into 120 rectangles 2" x 6$\frac{1}{2}$".
3. Cut 8 strips 2$\frac{3}{8}$" wide. Cut into 120 squares 2$\frac{3}{8}$". Cut these once diagonally to yield 240 half-square triangles.

Binding

Cut 10 strips 2$\frac{1}{2}$" wide.

PIECING AND ASSEMBLY

Blocks

1. With the marked 1$\frac{1}{4}$ yds. of Fabric A (background) and the 1$\frac{1}{4}$ yds. of Fabric C (accent) right sides together, stitch a $\frac{1}{4}$" seam on each side of diagonal lines. You will need 480 of these triangle units. When pressed, these units should measure 2" from raw edge to raw edge.

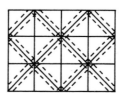

2. For each block, sew 2 triangle units going 1 direction and 2 triangles going the opposite direction:

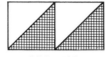 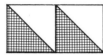

Make 120   Make 120

Add 1 pair to the 3¹/₂" center block. Add a Fabric A (background) square to the other pair; add to center block:

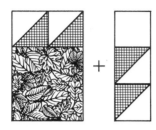

3. Add the 5" and 6¹/₂" strips of Fabric D (stem) to block:

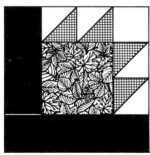

4. Sew triangle of Fabric D (stem) to end of trapezoids; add to block:

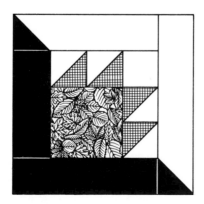

5. Following quilt diagram on page 40, assemble quilt top.

Borders and Finishing

1. Add first border. Piece the 2¹/₂" wide strips of Fabric C (accent) on the slant and measure off 2 strips, each 75¹/₂" long. Sew to top and bottom. Press. Measure off 2 strips, each 94¹/₄" long, and sew to long sides. Press.
2. Add second border. Piece the 3¹/₂" wide strips of Fabric B (main) on the slant and measure off 2 strips, each 79¹/₂" long. Sew to top and bottom. Press. Measure off 2 strips, each 100¹/₂" long, and sew to long sides. Press.
3. Layer, quilt, and bind.

Sawtooth Flower by Trudie Hughes, Elm Grove, Wisconsin, 1989, 85" x 100". By turning the blocks on each other, an interesting setting develops.

Sawtooth Flower by Trudie Hughes, Elm Grove, Wisconsin, 1989, 74" x 106". This delightful twin pastel quilt has a different setting.

California Twist by Trudie Hughes, Elm Grove, Wisconsin, 1989, 57" square. This wall hanging will certainly make a statement at Christmas. Hand quilted by Beverly Payne.

California Star by Trudie Hughes, Elm Grove, Wisconsin, 1989, 43" square. This traditional version will please blue-and-white lovers.

Star in Heaven by Trudie Hughes, Elm Grove, Wisconsin, 1989, 84" x 101". A dark background highlights the other prints in this quilt.

Star in Heaven by Trudie Hughes, Elm Grove, Wisconsin, 1989, 84" x 101". A light background in this quilt brightens the design.

Star in Heaven by Trudie Hughes, Elm Grove, Wisconsin, 1989, 64" x 81". A bold paisley and contrasting prints dramatize this charming coverlet.

Star in Heaven by Trudie Hughes, Elm Grove, Wisconsin, 1989, 64" x 81". In this diagonally set quilt, the setting triangles are pieced, forming a pieced border look.

County Line by Trudie Hughes, Elm Grove, Wisconsin, 1989, 90" x 107". A striking combination of blues, along with an interesting pieced border, makes this quilt a winner.

County Line by Trudie Hughes, Elm Grove, Wisconsin, 1989, 60" x 78". These cheerful shades of red will sparkle any room.

County Line by Jan Genrich, New Berlin, Wisconsin, 1989, 60" x 78". Carefully shaded teal greens combine to create a dynamic effect.

County Line by Trudie Hughes, Elm Grove, Wisconsin, 1989, 38" x 53". What baby wouldn't like to cuddle in this soft pastel quilt?

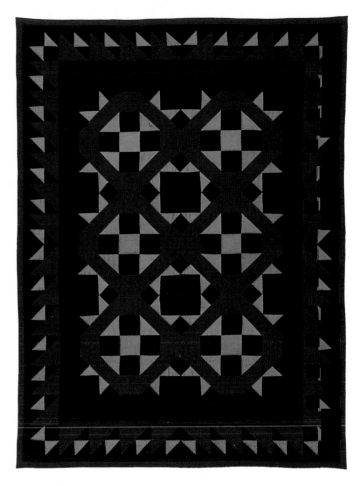

David and Goliath by Trudie Hughes, Elm Grove, Wisconsin, 1989, 37" x 49". Soft pastel colors are enhanced by a dramatic print border.

David and Goliath by Trudie Hughes, Elm Grove, Wisconsin, 1989, 33" x 45". Hand quilted by Mary Bronar. Dramatic Amish colors make a strong interpretation.

Banbury Cross by Trudie Hughes, Elm Grove, Wisconsin, 1989, 57" x 81". Navy and burgundy interplay to give visual interest to this quilt.

Banbury Cross by Trudie Hughes, Elm Grove, Wisconsin, 1989, 94" x 121". The large print is the main focus in this version.

Banbury Cross by Trudie Hughes, 1989, Elm Grove, Wisconsin, 58" square. The wonderful fish fabric creates the drama in this eye-catching quilt.

BANBURY CROSS

I saw this quilt in the Fall/Winter 1983 issue of *Quiltmaker* and knew I would have to make it. I was not surprised to find that it was designed by my most admired quilt designer, Judy Martin. I refigured the shapes to make it easier to cut with the rotary cutter. Your selection of fabric can greatly change the effect of the design. It can look either very contemporary or very traditional but looks especially striking when a large print is chosen for Fabric A.

Note: All quilts blocks in this quilt pattern are pieced the same way; they are simply pieced in two different color combinations. A great deal of time can be saved by piecing units, then assembling them.

Lesson: Piecing the featured unit; cutting parallelograms, half-square triangles, and quarter-square triangles; piecing quilt with diagonal set and pieced setting triangles.

Wall Hanging

Block size: 17"
Number of blocks: 5
Pieced area finishes to 48" square.
After first border, quilt will be 51" square.
After second border, quilt will be 58" square.

Fabric A
Fabric B
Fabric C
Fabric D
Fabric E

FABRIC REQUIREMENTS

45" wide fabric (see page 5)
Fabric A (background): 2½ yds. (1¾ yds. for
    piecing, ¾ yd. for last border)
Fabric B (main):1½ yds.
Fabric C (dark accent): ⅝ yd.
Fabric D (light accent): 1 yd. (½ yd. for piecing,
    ½ yd. for first border)
Fabric E (medium): 1 yd.
Backing: 3½ yds.
Binding: ¾ yd.

CUTTING INSTRUCTIONS

Fabric A (background)

1. Cut 2 strips 6⅞" wide. Cut into 8 squares 6⅞".
    Cut these once diagonally to yield 16 half-square
    triangles.

2. Cut 1 strip 7¼" wide. Cut into 4 squares 7¼".
    Cut with an **X** to yield 16 quarter-square tri-
    angles.

3. Cut 1 strip 25¼" wide. Make 4 cuts at 6½" and
    make a 45° cut at each end.

6½"

25¼"

4. Cut 2 squares 12⅞". Cut these once diagonally
    to yield the 4 corners.
5. Cut 6 strips 4" wide for last border.

Fabric B (main)

1. Cut 5 strips 2⅝" wide. With strips folded in half,
    cut 32 parallelograms, measuring cuts at 5". You
    should be able to get 6 from 1 strip. Remember
    to have strips right sides together to get mirror
    images.

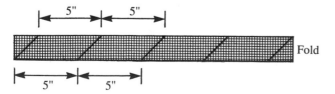

5"   5"

Fold

5"   5"

You should have 16 going one way and 16 going the
other way:

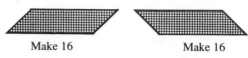

Make 16   Make 16

2. Cut 1 strip 2" wide. Cut into 16 squares 2".
3. Cut 1 strip 2⅜" wide. Cut into 16 squares 2⅜".
    Cut these once diagonally to yield 32 half-square
    triangles.

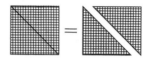

4. Cut 4 squares 5⅛" wide. Cut these once diago-
    nally to yield 8 half-square triangles.

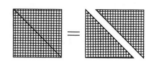

5. Cut 4 squares 3½" wide. Using the 1½" Speedy
    on the Rotary Mate™, remove 2 adjacent
    corners.

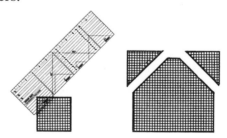

Fabric C (dark accent)

1. Cut 1 strip 5⅛" wide. Cut into 4 squares 5⅛".
    Cut these once diagonally to yield 8 half-square
    triangles.

2. Cut 4 squares 2".
3. Cut 1 strip 2⅜" wide. Cut into 4 squares 2⅜".
    Cut these once diagonally to yield 8 half-square
    triangles.

4. Cut 4 squares 3½".

Fabric D (light accent)

1. Cut 1 strip 3" wide. Cut into 8 squares 3". Cut these once diagonally to yield 16 half-square triangles.

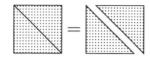

2. Cut 1 strip 3³/₈" wide. Cut into 8 squares 3³/₈". Cut these with an **X** to yield 32 quarter-square triangles.

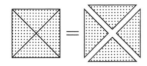

3. Cut 1 strip 7¹/₄" wide. Cut into 2 squares 7¹/₄". Cut with an **X** to yield 8 quarter-square triangles.

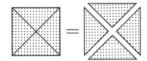

4. With the remaining fabric from step 3, cut 2 squares 6⁷/₈". Cut these once diagonally to yield 4 half-square triangles.

5. Cut 1 square 3¹/₂".
6. Cut 7 strips 2" wide for first border.

Fabric E (medium)

1. Cut 2 squares 3³/₈". Cut these with an **X** to yield 8 quarter-square triangles.

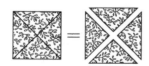

2. Cut 2 squares 3". Cut these once diagonally to yield 4 half-square triangles.

3. Cut 3 strips 2⁵/₈" wide. With strips folded in half, cut 16 parallelograms, measuring cuts at 5".

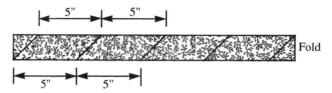

You should have 8 going one way and 8 going the other way:

Make 8   Make 8

4. Cut 2 strips 3¹/₂" wide. Cut into 16 squares 3¹/₂". Using the 1¹/₂" Speedy on the Rotary Mate™, remove 2 adjacent corners.

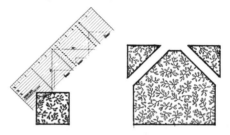

5. Cut 1 strip 5¹/₈" wide. Cut into 4 squares 5¹/₈". Cut these once diagonally to yield 8 half-square triangles.

PIECING AND ASSEMBLY

Blocks

1. Make 16 units that look like this:

and 4 units that look like this:

2. Make 16 units that look like this:

and 4 units that look like this:

3. Assemble 4 center A blocks:

Assemble 1 center B block.

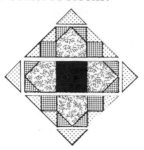

4. Add large triangles to all blocks:

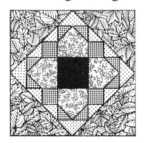 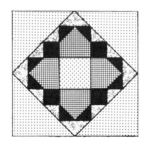

5. Make 8 triangle units that look like this:

Make 8 triangle units that look like this:

and 8 triangle units that look like this:

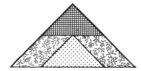

Add these to blocks and "decapitated triangles":

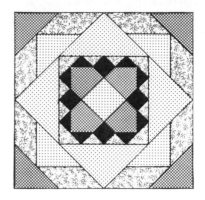

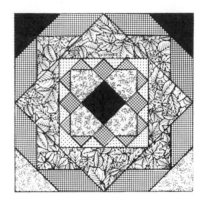

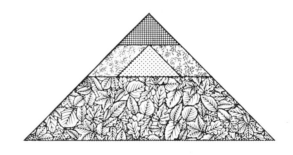

6. Starting in a corner and following quilt diagram on page 57, assemble in rows.
7. Add corners.

Borders and Finishing
1. After pieced area is completed, add first border. Piece the 2" strips of Fabric D (light accent) on the slant and measure off 2 strips, each 48½" long; sew to 2 sides. Press. Measure off 2 strips, each 51½" long, and sew to remaining sides. Press.
2. Add last border. Piece the 4" wide strips of Fabric A (background) on the slant and measure off 2 strips, each 51½" long; sew to first 2 sides. Press. Measure off 2 strips, each 58½" long, and sew to remaining sides. Press.
3. Layer, quilt, and bind.

Lap Quilt

Block size: 17"
Number of blocks: 8
Pieced area finishes to 48" x 72".
After first border, quilt will be 51" x 75".
After last border, quilt will be 57" x 81".

Fabric A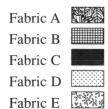
Fabric B
Fabric C
Fabric D
Fabric E

FABRIC REQUIREMENTS

45" wide fabric (see page 5)
Fabric A (background): 3¼ yds. (2¼ yds. for piecing, 1 yd. for last border)
Fabric B (main): 1¾ yds. (1¼ yd. for piecing, ½ yd. for first border)
Fabric C (dark accent): ½ yd.
Fabric D (light): 1 yd.
Fabric E (medium): 1¼ yds.
Backing: 5 yds.
Binding: ¾ yd.

CUTTING INSTRUCTIONS

Fabric A (background)

1. Cut 3 strips 6⅞" wide. Cut into 12 squares 6⅞". Cut these once diagonally to yield 24 half-square triangles.

2. Cut 2 strips 7¼" wide. Cut into 6 squares 7¼". Cut with an X to yield 24 quarter-square triangles.

3. Cut 1 strip 25¼" wide. Make 6 cuts at 6½" and make a 45° cut at each end.

4. Cut 2 squares 12⅞". Cut these once diagonally to yield the 4 corners.
5. Cut 7 strips 3½" wide for last border.

Fabric B (main)

1. Cut 8 strips 2⅝" wide. With strips folded in half, cut 48 parallelograms, measuring cuts at 5". You should be able to get 6 from 1 strip. Remember to have strips right sides together to get mirror images.

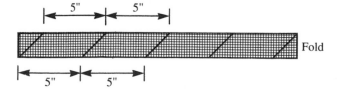

You should have 24 going one way and 24 going the other way:

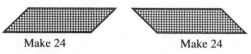

2. Cut 2 strips 2" wide. Cut into 24 squares 2".
3. Cut 2 strips 2⅜" wide. Cut into 24 squares 2⅜". Cut these once diagonally to yield 48 half-square triangles.

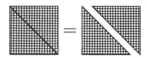

4. Cut 1 strip 5⅛" wide. Cut into 7 squares 5⅛". Cut these once diagonally to yield 14 half-square triangles.

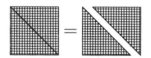

5. Cut 1 strip 3½" wide. Cut into 8 squares 3½". Using the 1½" Speedy on the Rotary Mate™, remove 2 adjacent corners.

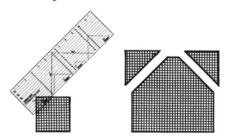

6. Cut 7 strips 2" wide for first border.

Fabric C (dark accent)

1. Cut 1 strip 5⅛" wide. Cut into 7 squares 5⅛". Cut these once diagonally to yield 14 half-square triangles.

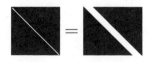

2. Cut 1 strip 2" wide. Cut into 8 squares 2".
3. Cut 1 strip 2⅜" wide. Cut into 8 squares 2⅜". Cut these once diagonally to yield 16 half-square triangles.

4. Cut 1 strip 3½" wide. Cut into 6 squares 3½".

Fabric D (light)

1. Cut 1 strip 3" wide. Cut into 12 squares 3". Cut these once diagonally to yield 24 half-square triangles.

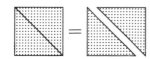

2. Cut 1 strip 3⅜" wide. Cut into 12 squares 3⅜". Cut these with an X to yield 48 quarter-square triangles.

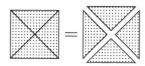

3. Cut 1 strip 6⅞" wide. Cut into 4 squares 6⅞". Cut these once diagonally to yield 8 half-square triangles.

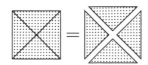

4. Cut 1 strip 7¼" wide. Cut into 4 squares 7¼". Cut with an X to yield 14 quarter-square triangles.

5. Cut 2 squares 3½".

Fabric E (medium)

1. Cut 1 strip 3⅜" wide. Cut into 4 squares 3⅜". Cut these with an X to yield 16 quarter-square triangles.

2. Cut 4 squares 3". Cut these once diagonally to

yield 8 half-square triangles.

3. Cut 5 strips 2⅝" wide. With strips folded in half, cut 28 parallelograms, measuring cuts at 5".

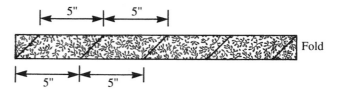
Fold

You should have 14 going 1 way and 14 going the other way:

Make 14   Make 14

4. Cut 2 strips 3½" wide. Cut into 24 squares 3½". Using the 1½" Speedy on the Rotary Mate™, remove 2 adjacent corners.

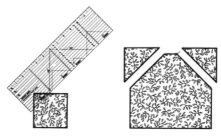

5. Cut 1 strip 5⅛" wide. Cut into 5 squares 5⅛". Cut these once diagonally to yield 10 half-square triangles.

Binding
Cut 8 strips 2½" wide.

PIECING AND ASSEMBLY

Blocks
1. Make 24 units that look like this:

and 8 units that look like this:

2. Make 24 units that look like this:

and 8 units that look like this:

3. Assemble 6 center A blocks and 2 center B blocks.

4. Add large triangles to all blocks:

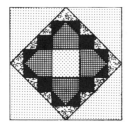 

5. Make 10 triangle units that look like this:

and 14 triangle units that look like this:

and 14 triangle units that look like this:

6. Add these triangle units to the blocks and "de-capitated triangles":

Make 4

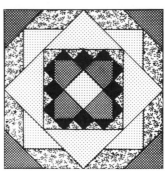

Make 2

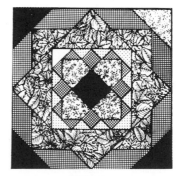

Make 2

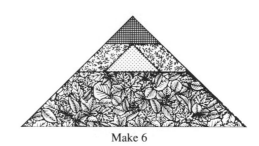

Make 6

7. Starting in a corner and following illustration on page 61, assemble in rows.
8. Add corners.

Borders and Finishing

1. After piecing is completed, add first border. Piece the 2" strips of Fabric B (main) on the slant and measure off 2 strips, each 48½" long; sew to top and bottom. Press. Measure off 2 strips, each 75½" long, and sew to long sides. Press.

2. Add last border. Piece the 3½" wide strips of Fabric A (background) on the slant and measure off 2 strips, each 51½" long; sew to top and bottom. Press. Measure off 2 strips, each 81½" long, and sew to long sides. Press.

3. Layer, quilt, and bind.

Part of the block in this quilt is repeated in the pieced border.

Large Quilt

Block size: 17"
Number of blocks: 18
Pieced area finishes to 72" x 96".
After first border, quilt will be 76" x 103".
After second border, quilt will be 81" x 108".
After pieced border, quilt will be 90" x 117".
After last border, quilt will be 94" x 121".

Fabric A   Fabric D ▢

Fabric B ▨   Fabric E ▨

Fabric C ■   Fabric F ▨

FABRIC REQUIREMENTS

45" wide fabric (see page 5)
Fabric A (background): 4³/₄ yds. (3³/₄ yds. for
    piecing, 1 yd. for last border)
Fabric B (main): 4 yds. (2¹/₄ yds. for piecing, 1 yd.
    for second border, ³/₄ yd. for pieced border)
Fabric C (dark accent): 2¹/₈ yds. (1¹/₈ yds. for piec-
    ing, 1 yd. for first border)
Fabric D (light): 1¹/₄ yds.
Fabric E (light accent): 2¹/₄ yds. (¹/₂ yd. for piecing,
    1³/₄ yds. for pieced border)
Fabric F (medium): 2¹/₄ yds. (1³/₄ yds. for piecing,
    ¹/₂ yd. for pieced border)
Backing: 10¹/₂ yds.
Binding: 1 yd.

CUTTING INSTRUCTIONS

Fabric A (background)

1. Cut 4 strips 6⁷/₈" wide. Cut into 24 squares 6⁷/₈".
   Cut these once diagonally to yield 48 half-square
   triangles.

2. Cut 3 strips 7¹/₄" wide. Cut into 12 squares 7¹/₄".
   Cut with an X to yield 48 quarter-square triangles.

3. Cut 2 strips 25¹/₄" wide. Cut 10 strips lengthwise
   6¹/₂" wide. Make diagonal cuts at both ends to
   make 10 "decapitated triangles."

4. Cut 2 squares 12⁷/₈". Cut these once diagonally
   to yield the 4 corners.
5. Cut 11 strips 2¹/₂" wide for last border.

Fabric B (main)

1. Cut 16 strips 2⁵/₈" wide. With strips folded in
   half, cut 96 parallelograms, measuring cuts at 5".
   You should be able to get 6 from 1 strip. Re-

member to have strips right sides together to get
mirror images.

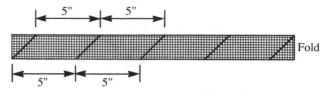

You should have 48 going 1 direction and 48 going
the opposite direction:

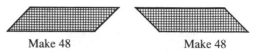

Make 48   Make 48

2. Cut 3 strips 2" wide. Cut into 48 squares 2".
3. Cut 3 strips 2³/₈" wide. Cut into 48 squares 2³/₈".
   Cut these once diagonally to yield 96 half-square
   triangles.

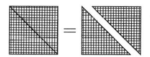

4. Cut 3 strips 5¹/₈" wide. Cut into 17 squares
   5¹/₈". Cut these once diagonally to yield 34
   half-square triangles.

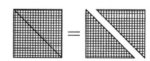

5. Cut 2 strips 3¹/₂" wide. Cut into 24 squares 3¹/₂".
   Using the 1¹/₂" Speedy on the Rotary Mate™,
   remove 2 adjacent corners.

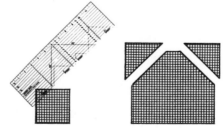

6. Cut 10 strips 3" wide for second border.

For pieced border:
1. Cut 5 strips 2" wide. Cut into 84 squares 2".
2. Cut 3 strips 2³/₈" wide. Cut into 42 squares 2³/₈".
   Cut these once diagonally to yield 84 half-square
   triangles.

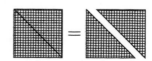

3. Cut 2 strips 3" wide. Cut into 21 squares 3". Cut once diagonally to yield 42 half-square triangles.

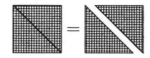

Fabric C (dark accent)

1. Cut 4 strips 5⅛" wide. Cut into 24 squares 5⅛". Cut these once diagonally to yield 48 half-square triangles.

2. Cut 2 strips 2" wide. Cut into 24 squares 2".
3. Cut 2 strips 2⅜" wide. Cut into 24 squares 2⅜". Cut these once diagonally to yield 48 half-square triangles.

4. Cut 2 strips 3½" wide. Cut into 12 squares 3½".
5. Cut 4 strips 4" wide for first border.
6. Cut 6 strips 2½" wide for first border.

Fabric D (light)

1. Cut 2 strips 6⅞" wide. Cut into 12 squares 6⅞". Cut these once diagonally to yield 24 half-square triangles.

2. Cut 2 strips 7¼" wide. Cut into 9 squares 7¼". Cut with an X to yield 34 quarter-square triangles.

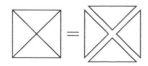

3. Cut 1 strip 3½" wide. Cut into 6 squares 3½".

Fabric E (light accent)

1. Cut 2 strips 3" wide. Cut into 24 squares 3". Cut these once diagonally to yield 48 half-square triangles.

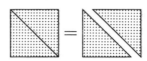

2. Cut 3 strips 3⅜" wide. Cut into 24 squares 3⅜". Cut these with an X to yield 96 quarter-square triangles.

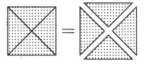

For pieced border:

1. Cut 4 strips 3⅜" wide. Cut into 42 squares 3⅜". Cut with an X to yield 168 quarter-square triangles.

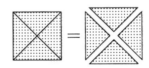

2. Cut 3 strips 10¼" wide. Cut into 10 squares 10¼". Cut with an X to yield 38 quarter-square triangles.

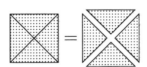

3. Cut 2 squares 9⅞". Cut these once diagonally for the corners.

Fabric F (medium)

1. Cut 1 strip 3" wide. Cut into 12 squares 3". Cut these once diagonally to yield 24 half-square triangles.

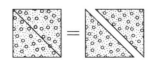

2. Cut 1 strip 3⅜" wide. Cut into 12 squares 3⅜". Cut these with an **X** to yield 48 quarter-square triangles.

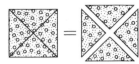

3. Cut 12 strips 2⅝" wide. With strips folded in half, cut 68 parallelograms, measuring cuts at 5".

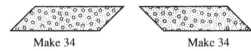

You should have 34 going 1 direction and 34 going the opposite direction:

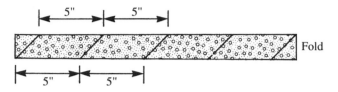

4. Cut 4 strips 3½" wide. Cut into 48 squares 3½". Using the 1½" Speedy on the Rotary Mate™, remove 2 adjacent corners.

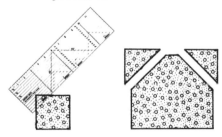

For pieced border:
   Cut 4 strips 3½" wide. Cut into 42 squares 3½". Using the 1½" Speedy on the Rotary Mate™, remove 2 adjacent corners.

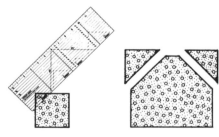

Binding
Cut 12 strips 2½" wide.

PIECING AND ASSEMBLY

Blocks
1. Piece 48 units that look like this:

 Make 48

and 24 units that look like this:

 Make 24

2. Make 48 units that look like this:

 Make 48

and 24 units that look like this: Make 24

3. Assemble 12 center A blocks and 6 center B blocks.

4. Add 4 corners to each block:

5. Assemble 48 triangle units that look like this:

Make 48

and 34 triangle units that look like this:

Make 34

Add these triangle units to blocks and "decapitated triangles."

Make 12

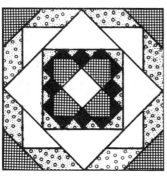

Make 6

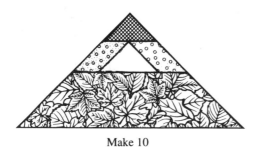

Make 10

6. Starting in a corner and following quilt diagram on page 66, assemble in rows.
7. Add corners.

Borders and Finishing

1. Add first border. Piece the 4" wide strips of Fabric C (dark accent) on the slant and measure off 2 strips, each 72½" long; sew to top and bottom. Press. Piece the 2½" wide strips of Fabric C (dark accent) and measure off 2 strips, each 103½" long; sew to long sides. Press.
2. Add second border. Piece the 3" strips of Fabric B (main) and measure off 2 strips, each 76½" long. Sew to top and bottom; press. Measure off 2 strips, each 108½" long, and sew to long sides. Press.
3. Add the pieced and last borders, if desired (see CREATIVE OPTION); layer, quilt, and bind.

CREATIVE OPTION

After the second border, you may add the pieced border.

1. Make 42 units that look like this:

Make 42

2. Alternating these units with the quarter-square triangles of Fabric C (light accent), sew 2 border strips of 9 units each. Sew these to top and bottom; press. Sew 2 border strips of 12 units each and sew to long sides. Press.
3. Add the corners.
4. Piece the 2½" wide strips of Fabric A (background) on the slant and measure off 2 strips, each 89½" long; sew to top and bottom. Press. Measure off 2 strips, each 122½" long; sew to long sides. Press.

Borders

PLAIN BORDERS

All plain borders for the quilt patterns in this book are planned to be cut on the crosswise grain. Therefore, the number of strips needed for a plain border is specified in the cutting instructions. If you want to cut your borders lengthwise, disregard these instructions and add to the yardage required.

If strips for the border are to be pieced, don't piece them with the short ends together. Instead, lay them in an L shape and sew in a diagonal line from one point of intersection to the opposite point of intersection.

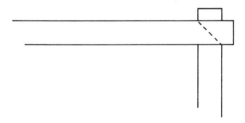

This slanted seam is more difficult to spot.

To piece border strips, sew all strips together and measure off the desired length. This will result in seams falling in different places on the quilt, making them harder to detect, as well. The only time I worry about where the seams fall is when they get too close to the corners.

I have designed the borders to be cut to length and sewn on blunted. I find, especially in handling pieced borders, that the quilt stays more "squared" with this type border. If you are not careful with mitered borders, the outside dimensions may differ. However, if you do prefer to miter your borders, you will have to cut more strips and add on to the planned yardage. I find the best way to sew on these borders is to establish the center of both the border and the quilt, then match ends and centers.

Several of the quilts in this book have pieced borders. These are not necessary if you do not want to tackle them; just make plain borders instead.

PIECED BORDERS

Pieced borders can add interest to a quilt. Quilts that have a lot of empty space, such as those set diagonally, are good candidates. My method of planning pieced borders is to determine the size of the pieced border and build up the quilt to fit it. Planning a spacer border, after the pieced area of your quilt and before your pieced border, will accomplish two things:

1. If you have a busy quilt, a spacer border gives relief before the pieced border.
2. The spacer border will make the pieced border mathematically compatible to the pieced area.

You will find many pieced border ideas in all of my *Template-Free Quiltmaking* books. I have also included a Border Ideas section in this book (see page 75). You may want to repeat some portion of the block itself, or some of the same shapes.

I have developed ten simple steps, which should be helpful in the planning of a pieced border. If you are putting the pieced border onto a square, you will need to go through these steps only once. However, if you are planning to put it onto a rectangle, you will have to follow these steps for the width and then go through them again for the length.

Step 1. Determine the finished dimensions of your quilt. The ultimate goal of this step is to have the two opposite sides of your quilt measure the same. If you are careful in your piecing, this shouldn't be a problem. In the quilt patterns from all my books, you will find these numbers near the beginning of the pattern, i.e., "Pieced area finishes to . . . " Either figure your dimensions by adding up finished block measurements or carefully measure. If the two sides do not measure the same, you will need to make adjustments.

Step 2. Determine the size of the repeating unit. This can be adjusted by changing the size of the pieces used in the unit.

Step 3. Determine whether the border requires an odd or even number of units. Your main concern should be how the border will go around the corners. If a pieced border reverses in the middle of the quilt, it will require an even number of units.

Sometimes a unit is split in half, and each half is used, one on each end. In this instance, you will also need an even number of units.

If a pieced border alternates two different units, you will need to plan an odd number of units to fit a side, so the same unit will be on each end.

Some pieced borders have a turning unit. This unit differs from the other units and usually appears in the center of the pieced border. An even number of units will be on each side of this unit, but its presence will mean an odd number of units in the border.

Many borders do not have these limitations and can have any number of units:

Step 4. Divide the quilt measurement (step 1) by the unit measurement (step 2). This step will give you the approximate number of units you will need.

Step 5. Determine the number of units that will yield a measurement larger than the finished quilt top. You need to come up with the next workable number from step 4 that allows at least a ³/₄" border. This will determine the size of the spacer border needed. If an even number is required, go up to the next workable even number. If an odd number is required, go up to the next workable odd number.

Step 6. Multiply the number of units needed from step 5 by the unit measurement (step 2). This will give you the measurement of the pieced border. The spacer border will build the quilt measurement up to this measurement.

Step 7. Subtract the finished measurement of the quilt (step 1) from the pieced border measurement (step 6). This is the total amount needed to build the quilt up to the right measurement.

Step 8. Divide by 2. When you divide the total amount needed by 2, you will have the finished measurement for each side of the spacer border.

Step 9. Add ¹/₄" seam allowance for each side. By adding ¹/₂" (total) seam allowance, you will know how wide to cut the spacer border strips.

Step 10. To allow for the spacer border strips sewn to the top and bottom, use measurement computed in step 6, plus ¹/₂". Sew these strips onto the sides that need expanding. If you need to expand the width of the quilt, sew these strips onto the long sides of the quilt; if you need to expand the length of the quilt, sew these strips onto the short sides of the quilt.

Do not be surprised if the numbers for the spacer border do not come out the same for both the length and the width of your quilt. It is not uncommon for the spacer border to be one size for the width of the quilt and a different size for the length. You usually are not aware of this discrepancy once the pieced border is on.

If you need an especially large spacer border, you can divide it into two borders, making the first border uneven and the second border the same measurement all around.

I prefer to use squared borders rather than mitered ones. I find that the squared borders stabilize the pieced area of the quilt. If you do not properly apply mitered borders, you can add unplanned inches to the measurement of your quilt.

To help you go through these steps, I have included a work sheet on page 73, for you to jot in your numbers as you plan your borders. You will want to photocopy this work sheet, so you will have one for each quilt that you plan to make.

You will probably find a calculator helpful in figuring the numbers for your border.

Decimal Equivalents to Fractions (rounded up to two decimal points)

¹/₈" = .13	¹/₂" = .5	³/₄" = .75
¹/₄" = .25	⁵/₈" = .63	⁷/₈" = .88
³/₈" = .38		

BORDER WORK SHEET

Border for top and bottom of quilt:

1. Finished quilt measures _____ long.

2. Size of repeating unit _____

3. Odd or even number of units _____

4. Divide quilt measurement (step 1) by unit measurement (step 2). _____

5. Next workable odd or even number of units, depending on requirement from step 3 _____

6. Multiply number from step 5 by unit measurement (step 2). _____

7. Subtract quilt measurement (step 1) from finished measurement of pieced border (step 6). _____

8. Divide by 2. _____

9. Add $\frac{1}{4}$" seam allowance for each side ($\frac{1}{2}$" total). _____
   Cut border strips this width.

10. Use the finished width measurement of the quilt, plus $\frac{1}{2}$", for cutting the length of these strips. _____
    Sew onto top and bottom.

Border for long sides of quilt:

1. Finished quilt measures _____ wide.

2. Size of repeating unit _____

3. Odd or even number of units _____

4. Divide quilt measurement (step 1) by unit measurement (step 2). _____

5. Next workable odd or even number, depending on your requirement from step 3 _____

6. Multiply number from step 5 by unit measurement (step 2). _____

7. Subtract quilt measurement (step 1) from finished measurement of pieced border (step 6). _____

8. Divide by 2. _____

9. Add $\frac{1}{4}$" seam allowance for each side ($\frac{1}{2}$" total). _____
   Cut each border strip this width.

10. Use the finished length of the border strip (step 6 from first column), plus $\frac{1}{2}$", for cutting the length of these strips. _____
    Sew these strips onto the long sides.

Let's use an example and put the Judy's Star border onto the Woven Hearts quilt. But this time we will use a smaller repeated unit (2½") and we will reverse it in the middle.

Border for top and bottom of quilt:
1. Finished quilt measures 39½" long.
2. Size of repeating unit 2½"
3. Odd or even number of units even
4. Divide quilt measurement (step 1) by unit measurement (step 2). 39½" ÷ 2½" = 15.8
5. Next workable odd or even number of units 18 (we need an even number)
6. Multiply number from step 5 by unit measurement (step 2). 18 x 2½" = 45"
7. Subtract quilt measurement (step 1) from finished measurement of pieced border (step 6). 45" − 39.5" = 5½"
8. Divide by 2. 5½" ÷ 2 = 2¾"
9. Add ¼" seam allowance for each side (½" total). 2¾" + ½" = 3¼" Cut border strips this width.
10. Use the finished width measurement of the quilt, plus ½" for cutting the length of these strips. 29½" + ½" = 30" Sew onto top and bottom.

Border for long sides of quilt:
1. Finished quilt measures 29½" wide.
2. Size of repeating unit 2½"
3. Odd or even number of units even
4. Divide quilt measurement (step 1) by unit measurement (step 2). 29½" ÷ 2½" = 11.8
5. Next workable odd or even number of units 14 (we need an even number)
6. Multiply number from step 5 by unit measurement (step 2). 14 x 2½" = 35"
7. Subtract quilt measurement (step 1) from finished measurement of pieced border (step 6). 35" − 29½" = 5½"
8. Divide by 2. 5½" ÷ 2 = 2¾"
9. Add ¼" seam allowance for each side (½" total). 2¾" + ½" = 3¼" Cut the border strips this width.
10. Use the finished measurement of pieced border (step 6) for top and bottom of quilt, plus ½", for cutting the length of these strips. 45" + ½" = 45½" Sew these strips onto the long sides.

In the previous example, all four border strips were cut the same width. Let's look at a border with different widths. In putting the Woven Hearts wall hanging border onto the Flying Geese in the Cabin lap quilt, new problems arise. First of all, there is a turning unit, and it is reversed in the middle.

Border for top and bottom of quilt:
1. Finished quilt measures 60" long.
2. Size of repeating unit 2⅞"
3. Odd or even number of units odd
4. Divide quilt measurement (step 1) by unit measurement (step 2). 60" ÷ 2⅞" = 20⅞
5. Next workable odd or even number of units 23 (we need an odd number)
6. Multiply number from step 5 by unit measurement (step 2). 23 x 2⅞" = 66¼"
7. Subtract quilt measurement (step 1) from finished measurement of pieced border (step 6). 66¼" − 60" = 6¼"
8. Divide by 2. 6¼" ÷ 2 = 3⅛"
9. Add ¼" seam allowance for each side (½" total). 3⅛" + ½" = 3⅝" Cut border strips this width.
10. Use the finished width measurement of the quilt, plus ½", for cutting the length of these strips. 40" + ½" = 40½" Sew onto top and bottom.

Border for long sides of quilt:
1. Finished quilt measures 40" wide.
2. Size of repeating unit 2⅞"
3. Odd or even number of units odd (the turning unit, plus an even number of units on each side of it)
4. Divide quilt measurement (step 1) by unit measurement (step 2). 40" ÷ 2⅞" = 13.88
5. Next workable odd or even number of units 15 (we need an odd number)
6. Multiply number from step 5 by unit measurement (step 2). 15 x 2.88" = 43.2"
7. Subtract quilt measurement (step 1) from finished measurement of pieced border (step 6). 43.2" − 40" = 3.2"
8. Divide by 2. 3.2" ÷ 2 = 1⅝"
9. Add ¼" seam allowance for each side (½" total). 1⅝" + ½" = 2⅛" Cut border strips this width.
10. Use the finished measurement of pieced border for top and bottom of the quilt (step 6), plus ½", for cutting the length of these strips. 66¼" + ½" = 66¾" Sew onto long sides of quilt.

BORDER IDEAS

Border #1

This border was used on the Judy's Star quilt from my first book, *Template-Free Quiltmaking* (page 87) and on the large Woven Hearts quilt from *Even More* (page 66).

3"

Shapes used:

1. Half-square triangles. Cut 3⁷/₈" squares once diagonally.

3⁷/₈"

2. Quarter-square triangles. Cut 4¹/₄" squares with an **X**.

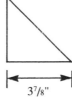

4¹/₄"

On the Woven Hearts quilt, the border units are reversed in the middle, an arrangement that requires an even number of units. The corners are plain squares.

On the Judy's Star quilt, all units are going in one direction around the quilt, so any number of units can be used. A separate corner unit is used.

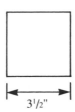

3¹/₂"

Border #2

I used this border on the Chimneys and Cornerstones quilts in *More Template-Free Quiltmaking* (pages 15 and 19). This border alternates two different pieced units, each measuring 3". When you alternate two different units, you need an odd number of units to ensure that both ends have the same unit to go around the corners.

 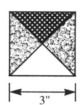

There are separate corner units:

Shapes used:
1. Quarter-square triangles. Cut $4^1/4$" squares, then cut with an X.

2. Half-square triangles. Cut $1^7/8$" squares once diagonally.

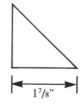

3. "Decapitated triangles". Cut $1^1/2$" wide strips, then make 45° cuts, going in opposite directions, every $4^1/4$".

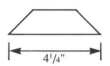

4. Rectangles. Cut $1^1/2$" x $3^1/2$".

5. Trapezoids. Cut from $1^1/2$" wide strips, cutting back at $2^7/8$".

6. Squares. Cut $1^1/2$" x $1^1/2$".

Border #3

Pinwheels in Pinwheels from *More Template-Free Quiltmaking* (pages 33 and 36) uses this border. It alternates two different units. Normally, that would mean you would need an odd number of units. In this case, one unit is split; therefore, an even number of units is required.

The corner is half of a unit.

Shapes used:
Half-square triangles. Make a 2⁷/₈" grid or cut triangles 2⁷/₈".

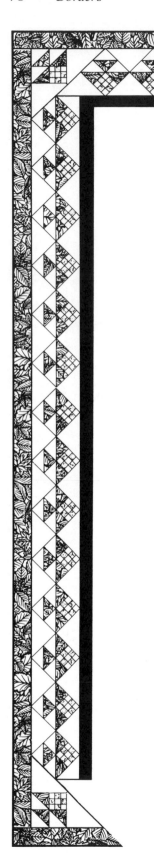

Border #4

The border on the Goose in the Pond quilt from *More Template-Free Quiltmaking* (page 39) repeated part of the block set diagonally. You can use any small block on point to get this effect. You need to know the diagonal measurement of the square that you will be setting diagonally.

$6^3/8"$

The small block that is set on point finishes to $4^1/2"$. The diagonal measurement is $6^3/8"$. You can use any number of units. There are four separate corners, which go on last.

Shapes used:

1. Small squares. Cut from $1^1/4"$ wide strips.

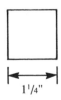

$1^1/4"$

2. Half-square triangles. Cut from a $3^1/8"$ grid.

$3^1/8"$

3. Quarter-square setting triangles. Cut $7^5/8"$ squares, then cut with an **X**.

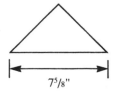

$7^5/8"$

Border #5

This stacked bricks border on the Farmer's Stepdaughter quilt from *More Template-Free Quiltmaking* (page 61) looks like Seminole piecing. However, in order to go around the corners, the border units need to reverse in the middle. This is accomplished with the help of a turning unit.

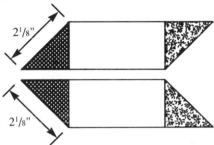

Use an even number of units on each side of a center turning unit.

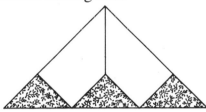

You will need to figure an odd number of units to account for the split triangle on the ends. At the ends of each border strip are separate end units:

These separate end units get sewn onto the last two border strips before they are added to the quilt.

Shapes used:

1. Rectangles. Cut 2" x $3^1/2$".

2. Quarter-square triangles. Cut $3^3/8$" squares with an **X**.

3. Trapezoids. Cut from 2" wide strips, cutting back at $3^7/8$".

4. "Decapitated triangles". Cut from 2" wide strip, cutting long side at $5^3/4$".

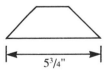

5. Squares. Cut 2" by 2".

6. Half-square triangles. Cut $1^7/8$" squares once diagonally.

Border #6

The border on the large Flying Geese in the Cabin quilt from *More Template-Free Quiltmaking* (page 72) repeats the shapes used in the quilt itself. The 3" unit is reversed in the middle, therefore requiring an even number of units.

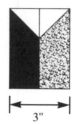

Separate corner units are added to the last two border strips before sewing to the quilt.

Shapes used:

1. Mirror-image trapezoids. Cut from 2" wide strips folded in half, cutting back at 4⁷/₈".

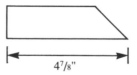

2. Half-square triangles. Cut 2³/₈" squares once diagonally.

3. Squares. Cut 3" x 3".

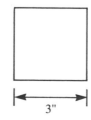

Border #7

The border on the lap size Flying Geese in the Cabin from *More Template-Free Quiltmaking* (page 77) uses the same pieced border as the larger quilt, only in a smaller scale.

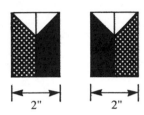

This border uses even numbers of units that are mirror images, reversing in the middle. Separate corner units are added to the last two border strips before sewing to the quilt.

Shapes used:

1. Trapezoids. Cut from $1^1/2$" wide strips, cutting back at $3^7/8$".

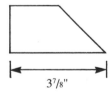

2. Half-square triangles. Cut $1^7/8$" squares once diagonally.

3. Squares. Cut $2^1/2$" x $2^1/2$".

Border #8

The Colorado Log Cabin quilt from *More Template-Free Quiltmaking* (page 81) uses mirror-image diamonds with triangles on the ends. The border reverses in the middle, so an even number of units is required.

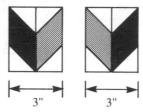

Separate corner units are added to the last two border strips before sewing to the quilt.

Shapes used:

1. Diamonds. Cut from 2" wide strips, making 45° cuts every 2".

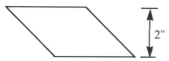

2. Half-square triangles. Cut $2^3/8$" squares once diagonally.

3. Squares. Cut $2^1/2$" x $2^1/2$".

Border #9

The border on the Evening in Ireland quilt from *Even More* (page 58) uses units made from strips. A quarter-square triangle has been added to the ends to stabilize the pieced border.

You can use any number of units on a side. Simply add end units to one end of each border strip.

The four corner units go on last.

Shapes used:
1. Squares. Cut from 2" wide strips sewn and subcut.

2. Quarter-square triangles. Cut 3⅜" squares with an X.

Border #10

The pieced border on the Woven Hearts wall hanging from *Even More* (page 60) is a challenge.

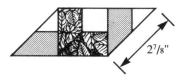

You will need an odd number of units, including a turning unit:

Use separate corner units.

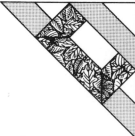

Shapes used:

1. Trapezoids. Fold fabric in half and cut 1$^1/_2$" wide strips, cutting back at 2$^7/_8$".

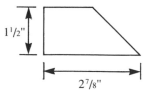

2. Quarter-square triangles. Cut 2$^5/_8$" squares with an X.

3. Squares. Cut 1$^1/_2$" x 1$^1/_2$".

4. Rectangles. Cut 1$^1/_2$" x 2$^1/_2$".

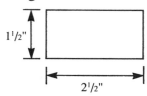

5. "Decapitated triangles". Cut from 1$^1/_2$" wide strips, cutting 45° angles in opposite directions, 5$^1/_4$" apart.

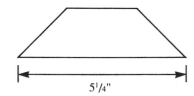

6. Half-square triangles. Cut 2$^1/_4$" squares once diagonally.

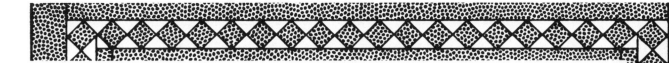

Border #11

The border on Road to St. Louis from *Even More* (page 69) is similar to the one on the Goose in the Pond quilt, with a small square, set diagonally. In this case, it is simply a plain small square. You need to work with its diagonal measurement.

You can use any number of units, but notice the split unit on the ends.

There is a separate corner unit:

Shapes used:
1. Squares. Cut 2" x 2".

2. Quarter-square triangles. Cut $3^3/8$" squares with an X.

3. Half-square triangles. Cut 2" squares once diagonally.

Border #12

Arrows revolve around the small This Way to My House quilt from *Even More* (page 80). These arrows are made up of flying geese units and a rail unit.

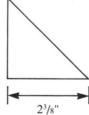

3"

Since all the arrows are heading the same way, you can use any number of units.

Shapes used:

1. Half-square triangles. Cut 2³/₈" squares once diagonally.

2³/₈"

2. Quarter-square triangles. Cut 4¹/₄" squares with an X.

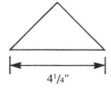

4¹/₄"

3. Rail units. Cut from 1¹/₂" wide sewn strips.

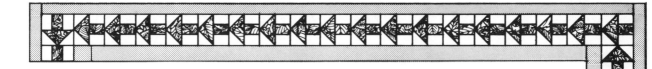

Border #13

The border on the large This Way to My House quilt from *Even More* (page 84) is the same as on the smaller one (Border #12), only in a different scale.

4"

You can use any number of units.

Shapes used:
1. Half-square triangles. Cut $2^7/_8$" squares once diagonally.

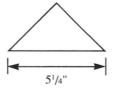

$2^7/_8$"

2. Quarter-square triangles. Cut $5^1/_4$" squares with an X.

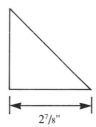

$5^1/_4$"

3. Rail units. Cut from $1^3/_4$" wide sewn strips.

Border #14

Feathered Star quilts from *Even More* (pages 88 and 91) use simple sawtooth borders made up of reversed half-square triangles. This border is also used on the Sawtooth Flower twin quilt in this book (page 36).

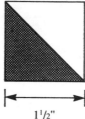

1½"

You will need an even number of units, since they reverse in the middle. The corner can be a plain square or another triangle unit.

Shapes used:

1. Half-square triangles. Cut from a 2³/₈" grid.

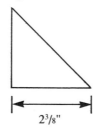

2³/₈"

2. Squares. Cut 2" x 2".

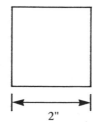

2"

Border #15

The border on the large County Line (page 10) uses a block set diagonally, except the setting triangles are also pieced with the featured unit.

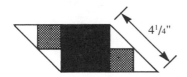

Any number of units can be used. There arc right end units and left end units.

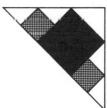

Separate corner units go on last.

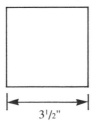

Shapes used:
1. Large squares. Cut 3$^1/_2$" x 3$^1/_2$".

2. Small squares. Cut 2" x 2".

3. Quarter-square triangles. Cut 3$^3/_8$" squares with an X.

4. Half-square triangles. Cut 3" squares once diagonally.

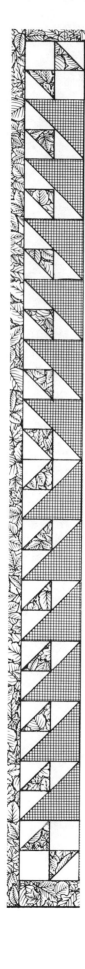

Border #16

The border on David and Goliath (page 13) uses a reversed unit. This unit is made up of the featured unit sewn to a triangle.

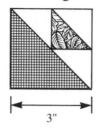

3"

You will need an even number of units, since they reverse in the middle. Separate corner units go on last.

Shapes used:

1. Large half-square triangles. Cut $3^{7}/_8$" squares once diagonally.

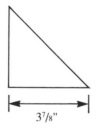

$3^{7}/_8$"

2. Small half-square triangles. Cut $2^{3}/_8$" squares or sew from a grid.

$2^{3}/_8$"

3. Squares. Cut 2" x 2".

2"

Border #17

The California Twist quilt (page 21) has a challenging pieced border, but it's worth the work. It alternates two mirror-image units and has a partial unit on one end.

Use an even number of units with an end unit on one side.

Corner units are added to the last two border strips before they are sewn on.

Shapes used:

1. Squares. Cut $2^5/8$" x $2^5/8$".

$2^5/8$"

2. Diamonds. Cut 2" wide strips with 45° cuts at 2".

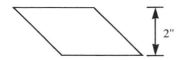

2"

3. Trapezoids. Cut 2" wide strips, cutting back at $4^1/2$".

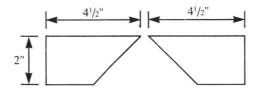

$4^1/2$" $4^1/2$" 2"

4. Rectangles. Cut 2" x $2^5/8$".

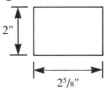

2" $2^5/8$"

5. Triangles. Cut $2^3/8$" squares once diagonally.

$2^3/8$"

6. Squares. Cut 2" x 2".

2"

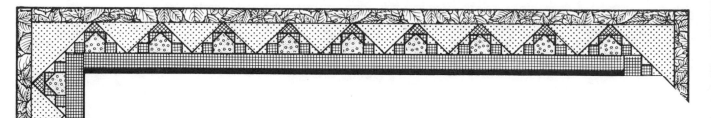

Border #18

The border on the large Banbury Cross (page 66) uses part of the block itself, so you will be working with diagonal measurements. The pieced unit alternates with a setting triangle.

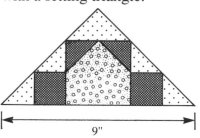

9"

You can use any number of units with plain corners.

Shapes used:

1. Squares. Cut 2" x 2".

2"

2. Half-square triangles. Cut $2^3/8$" squares once diagonally.

$2^3/8$"

3. Half-square triangles. Cut 3" squares once diagonally.

3"

4. Squares. Cut $3^1/2$" squares, cutting off two corners from each with a $1^1/2$" Speedy on the Rotary Mate™.

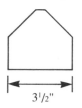

$3^1/2$"

5. Quarter-square triangles. Cut $3^3/8$" squares with an X.

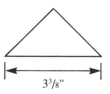

$3^3/8$"

6. Quarter-square triangles. Cut $10^1/4$" squares with an X.

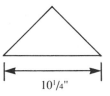

$10^1/4$"

7. Half-square triangles. Cut $9^7/8$" squares once diagonally.

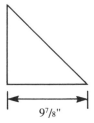

$9^7/8$"

Technique Review

TOOLS AND RULES

The secret to template-free quiltmaking is the equipment you use. With the right equipment and techniques, this type of quiltmaking can be as accurate as it is fast.

The first thing you will need is a rotary cutter. It comes in two sizes, but I recommend the larger cutter. It is much easier to use and gives you better control when cutting through multiple layers. The Olfa™ mat is the preferred surface for cutting because of its matte finish, which holds the fabric still and protects the blade. You will need at least an 18" x 24" mat.

The Rotary Rule™ and the Rotary Mate™ were developed for the techniques in my *Template-Free Series* of books. The Rotary Rule™ is divided into ¼" increments with solid lines and into ⅛" increments with dashes across its width, so you can measure right to left. With this feature, you can measure and cut at the end of the ruler. For more advanced procedures, the ruler has 45°-angle markings going both directions in the center of the ruler.

The Rotary Mate™ extends the larger ruler for wider cuts. More importantly, this unique ruler has "Speedies" along one edge to make Snowball blocks and similar shapes with ease. The Banbury Cross quilt uses this feature. The 12" length is also easy to handle. Once the fabric has been straightened and refolded, strips are easier to cut with the smaller ruler. For the smaller, more complex shapes, this ruler is a must.

In addition to these tools, I find a 12" right triangle very helpful. I like my fluorescent-colored one, because it is easier to find in a mess. These are very inexpensive.

It is so important to work with the best tools possible. "The right tool for the right job" is true. Short-cutting some of the tedious procedures in quilting lets you get to the more enjoyable parts faster.

The Rotary Rule™ and Rotary Mate™ are available through Patched Works, 13330 Watertown Plank Road, Elm Grove, Wisconsin 53122.

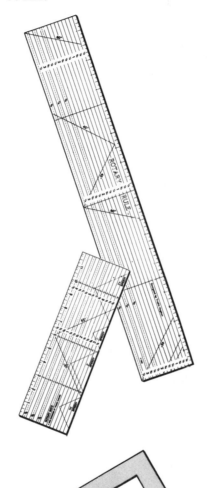

SLICE AND DICE

It is important to learn to use the rotary cutter accurately and efficiently. Since you want to work with straight pieces, you must learn to cut perfectly straight strips.

The first step is to straighten the fabric. Threads in fabric are often far from perpendicular these days, making it almost impossible to truly straighten fabric. So, we will be working with "close grain." You will need to make clean cuts, rather than cuts that are exactly on the straight of grain.

1. Fold fabric in half, selvage to selvage, the way it comes off the bolt.

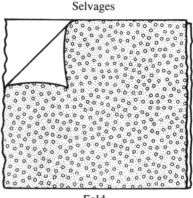

Selvages

Fold

2. Lay right triangle along folded edge of fabric and push against right side of ruler until you are just at the edge. (If you are right-handed, the bulk of the fabric should be coming from the right.)

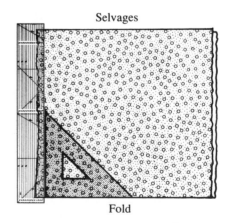

Selvages

Fold

3. Hold ruler down with your left hand and begin cutting slightly in front of the fold. Walk your hand up parallel with the cutter and continue to cut off the end of the fabric. If you try to hold on to the ruler at the bottom and cut to the end of it, you most likely will move it and therefore cut inaccurately. This is the only

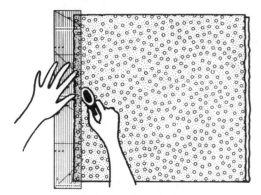

time you will have to cut such a long slice.

4. Then, fold the fabric one more time, lining up the cut edges. Using markings on ruler, cut appropriate strip width. Now you can make cuts only 11" long, which is much easier. Check about every 5 cuts to see that you are still straight. Open up fabric and use right triangle and ruler again to make sure you are still perpendicular with the first fold.

 If cuts are not perpendicular to the fold, strips will have V or W shapes when you open them up. Everything is cut selvage to selvage, so you will soon be aware of this.

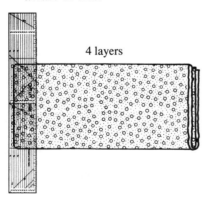

4 layers

Note: Cutting instructions have been written in the shortest possible form. When instructions tell you to "cut 5 strips 3" wide," this means each strip should be cut 3" wide.

 When you need to cut fabric strips wider than 3½", you can combine the width of ruler with any portion of the Rotary Mate™. You will find most cuts in this book are 3½" or less. If you have cuts wider than the two rulers combined, use

the side of the ruler to measure off desired width.

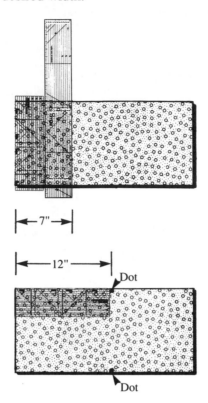

|← 7" →|

|← 12" →| Dot

    Dot

Squares and Rectangles

 Some designs will require independent squares or rectangles. These "loose" units will be cut from strips.

 Cut strips the required width. Then, working with at least four layers at a time, straighten left edge of strips (usually has selvages and maybe a fold) by placing cut edge on halfway line of ruler and making a perpendicular slice.

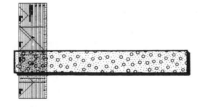

Then, measure left to right, cutting squares same width as strips.

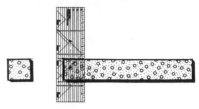

Rectangles are measured by using the long side of the ruler.

|← 6½" →|

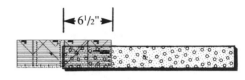

Triangles

Half-square triangles. A half-square triangle is half of a square and is measured on the two short sides. These sides are on grain.

 If you were to draft a triangle on graph paper and add a ¼" seam allowance all around, you would see that the difference between the finished edges of the triangle and the cut edges with the seam allowance is not what you might expect. The straight side has ¼" difference, yet the pointed side has ⅝" difference between the finished and the cut point. The formula for half-square triangles is the finished size plus ⅞".

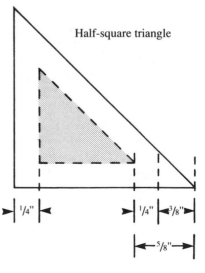

Half-square triangle

|← ¼" →| |← ¼" →|← ⅜" →|

|← ⅝" →|

¼" + ¼" + ⅜" = ⅞"

Cut a strip the desired measurement plus $^7/_8$". On the Rotary Rule™, the most common triangles are built in as dotted lines.

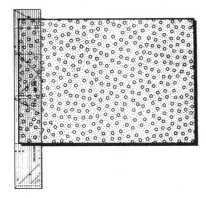

Then, subcut into squares with the same measurement.

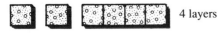

4 layers

Take a stack of four squares and cut once diagonally from corner to corner. These triangles are now the right size to mix with other shapes.

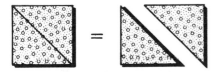

Quarter-square triangles. When a square is divided into four triangles, these triangles are referred to as quarter-square triangles. A quarter-square triangle is a right triangle that has the long side on grain. It is the measurement of the long side that will concern you. The outside edge of every square and the outside edge of every quilt is easier to handle if on grain, rather than on the bias, which can stretch.

If you draw a quarter-square triangle on graph paper, putting the long side on grain and drawing the seam allowance, you will find two points with $^5/_8$" sticking out from the finished points. The sum of these is

$1^1/_4$". So, the formula for dealing with a quarter-square triangle is the finished measurement of the long side plus $1^1/_4$".

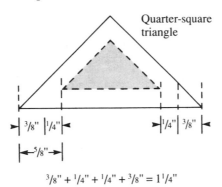

Quarter-square triangle

$^3/_8$" $^1/_4$" $^1/_4$" $^3/_8$"

$^5/_8$"

$^3/_8" + ^1/_4" + ^1/_4" + ^3/_8" = 1^1/_4"$

If quarter-square triangles are cut and used independently:

1. Cut a strip the desired width.

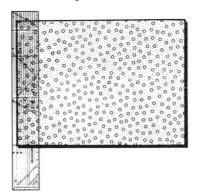

2. Subcut into squares with the same measurement.

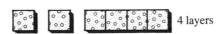

4 layers

With a stack of these squares (at least four), cut with an X by lining up the ruler and cutting from corner to corner. Without moving these pieces, cut in the other direction. Each square will yield four triangles with the long sides on grain.

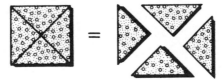

Trapezoids

Trapezoids share the same math as half-square triangles. To cut these, measure the finished length of the long side of the trapezoid, then add $^7/_8$".

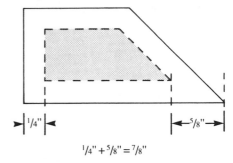

$^1/_4$" $^5/_8$"

$^1/_4" + ^5/_8" = ^7/_8"$

On some designs you will work with all strips right sides up and on some you will work with strips folded in half. Be sure to read instructions carefully.

Working with four layers at a time, cut left edge perpendicular with the top and bottom edges. From the left edge, measure the distance called for in the pattern and make a dot at the top edge, unless the pattern tells you otherwise.

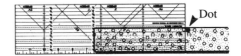

Dot

Cut with the 45° mark on the ruler, lining it up with the longer cut edge and stopping just short of the dot.

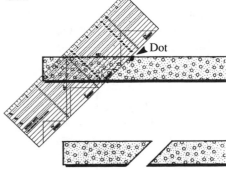

Dot

The next cut does not have to be marked. Measure the desired amount and make a straight cut.

"Decapitated Triangles"

Although this shape is really a trapezoid, I refer to it as a "decapitated triangle" to help you form a mental picture of the shape you will cut. These shapes remind me of a quarter-square triangle with its tip cut off. The math is the same: Measure the finished length of the long side and add $1^1/4$".

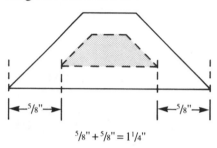

$$5/8" + 5/8" = 1^1/4"$$

Cut the required width strip. Using the Rotary Mate™, align the 45°-angle marking with the top edge of strip. Cut.

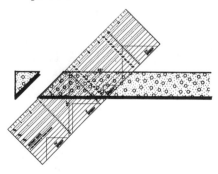

Measure along edge of strip until you get to desired length and make a dot.

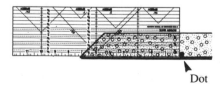

Dot

Line up ruler with dot and cut a 45° angle in the opposite direction.

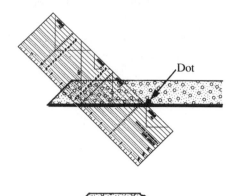

Dot

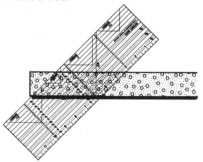

Diamonds

Cut the required width strip. Using the Rotary Mate™, line up the 45° angle with the longer cut edge to establish the first cut. Keeping the 45° angle on the longer cut edge, slide the ruler over until the numbers in the middle are lined up with desired cut.

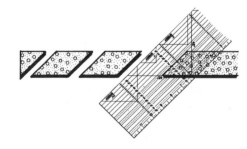

Subcutting Sewn Strips

Many designs begin merely as cut strips. These strips are sewn together, pressed, and then cut again. When subcutting, you can ensure accuracy by keeping the crossline of the ruler on a stitching line.

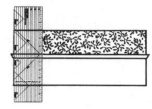

Four Patches are best pieced this way. To make a Four Patch, sew together two sets of contrasting strips. Press consistently toward the same color.

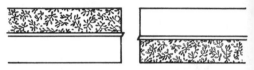

Then, place these two sets of sewn strips right sides together. Because of your pressing, you will find seam allowances already going in opposite directions.

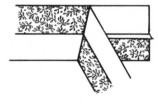

Trim the selvages off and cut in pairs from left to right. When you sew these pairs together, there is no need to match or layer; they are ready to feed through the sewing machine in chain fashion.

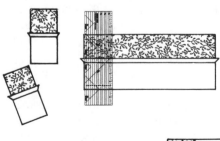

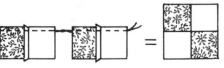

1 pair   Four Patch